Raising Peace:

Real-Life Strategies for Coparenting After Divorce

Susan Cook

ISBN: 978-1-0695106-0-0

To my children,

You were caught in the middle of something you never asked for, yet you had to live with the consequences every day.

This book, along with my decades of working with families, is my effort to break that cycle for others.

With all my love,

Mom

Author's Note

I am not a writer, but here I am, writing a book, hoping to make a difference.

What I hope you will find is a practical guide drawn from nearly 30 years of frontline experience supporting families through some of the most difficult chapters of their lives. It brings together the insight, tools, and real-world strategies I have used to help thousands of parents and children navigate separation, conflict, and change.

My path into this work was unexpected. I began by helping a criminally charged client with her family court case, and what I discovered stunned me. I had assumed that family court would be centered around supporting children, healing families, and promoting cooperation. Instead, I found a system that often inflamed conflict, delayed progress, and failed the very people it was meant to protect. I came to call it "the place where coparenting relationships go to die."

I had thought from the inside perspective it would be different. Just a few years earlier, I had gone through my own highly litigious divorce, right there in the same courthouse. I knew what it felt like to be caught up in the system, overwhelmed and uncertain, as a parent trying to navigate the financial and emotional elements of divorcing. However, now I was seeing how many other families were facing the same experience without enough support or guidance to get through it well.

Despite the system's shortcomings, I was effective with reaching quicker outcomes for my client, and so, I was invited to propose a permanent role, from which a career was born.

After several years in a frustratingly flawed system, I returned to school and became a mediator, arbitrator, and ultimately, a Certified Specialist-Parenting Coordinator. These roles allowed me to make an even greater impact working directly with separated parents, reducing harm, and creating more stability for children in two-home families.

Now, as I approach retirement, I feel the pull to keep helping. I have seen what works. I know what helps families move forward and what holds them back. I have poured as much of that knowledge into this book as I could.

This book is for parents who want to raise strong, secure children, even after separation.

I want to recognize that families come in many forms. Although I have used "mom and dad" for simplicity, this does not overlook the beautiful and diverse family structures I have encountered over the years or those who may be reading this book.

I also want you to know that I understand each family is unique and no solution is universal, so read with the understanding that you can take all, some, and adapt parts of what makes sense, especially in the Sample Parenting Plan at the end.

If even one family finds clarity, relief, or a better path forward through these pages, then writing this will have been worth it.

I hope that family is yours.

CONTENTS

An Introduction

Raising Peace: Real-Life Strategies for Coparenting After Divorce is a compassionate and practical guide for parents navigating the often-overwhelming terrain of post-divorce parenting from cooperative coparents to high-conflict, court-involved situations.

With over 20 years of frontline experience in family conflict resolution, Susan Cook has earned a nation-wide reputation for her work as a Certified Specialist-Parenting Coordinator and specialist in high-conflict cases. She is the developer of the **Family Court Worker** program; a groundbreaking initiative widely praised by judges and lawyers for its significant impact in reducing court time for families, especially those facing mental health challenges.

Blending professional insight with the lived experience of navigating divorce herself, Susan Cook offers deeply relatable guidance and proven strategies that help parents move from chaos to clarity. Her expertise lies in building parenting plans that go beyond logistics; they support the emotional well-being of children and provide a holistic foundation for healthier family dynamics.

Whether you are dealing with a cooperative coparent or entrenched conflict, **Raising Peace*: Real-Life Strategies for Coparenting After Divorce*** delivers real-life tools, thoughtful reflection, and a calm voice of reason to help you raise children with confidence, resilience, and peace.

Why This Book Matters

Separation and divorce may end a marriage, but it does not end parenting. For many families, it marks the beginning of a far more complex chapter, one that requires strength, grace, and a deep commitment to the well-being of your children. If you are reading this, you are likely navigating a terrain that can feel both isolating and overwhelming: how to coparent with someone you may no longer trust or understand, while still showing up every day for your children with love and consistency.

This book was written for you.

Whether you are early in the separation process or have been coparenting for years, the emotional weight of shared parenting after divorce is real. And yet, amid the conflict and confusion, there is also an opportunity, a chance to become the kind of parent your child needs most: steady, thoughtful, and deeply attuned to their emotional landscape.

You will not find perfection in these pages. Instead, you will find practical wisdom, gentle truths, and a clear-eyed approach to the real-life challenges coparents face. Each chapter offers guidance rooted in experience, compassion, and the firm belief that even in high-conflict situations, you can create a sense of safety and predictability for your children.

My hope is that this book will serve as your quiet companion. A place to return to when the noise gets loud. A reminder that you are not alone and that what you are doing matters deeply.

So, take a breath, settle in, and know this: parenting after divorce is not about winning. It is about healing, leading, and loving in ways that help your children feel secure in a world that may feel divided. You have already taken the first step just by opening this book.

Let's begin.

Chapter 1

What is Coparenting? How Do We Get There?

"Children do not need a perfect environment, they need a consistent one."

Coparenting is the quiet, ongoing decision to choose your child's future over your own past.

Effective coparenting speaks to the process of a combined effort by both parents to raise and support children, even if the parents are no longer in an intact relationship. It involves effective communication, compromise, and collaboration between both parents to create a stable and healthy environment in which children may thrive. It is a model of parenting that places the emotional, psychological, and developmental needs of children front and center.

Any two separated parents can technically be called coparents; effective coparenting is something more intentional, it is cooperative, respectful, and deeply rooted in a shared commitment to the child's well-being.

Key: Children deserve to THRIVE NOT JUST SURVIVE amidst their parents' separation and divorce.

What must be recognized from the outset is that effective coparenting has a profoundly positive impact, providing children with stability and a predictable environment. Coparenting can provide stability by ensuring that both parents are involved in not only all aspects of the children's lives but participating in and committed to their best interests. When this happens, the children receive the benefit of emotional grounding and are more likely to form secure attachments, both with their parents and with others. This involvement does not have to look the same for each parent, but the message it sends is consistent: "You are loved, you are safe, and we are here for you."

When both parents are not just active, but effective participants in all aspects of the children's lives, it allows the child access to the emotional and financial resources of both parents and provides them with two consistent environments of expectations. This means routines become easier, transitions between home become less distressing, and children gain the security of knowing their needs will be met, regardless of location. Predictability reduces anxiety, and children are better able to focus on their own development, friendships, schoolwork, and hobbies when they are not preoccupied with navigating between hostile parental dynamics.

Effective coparenting can also assist in reducing conflict between the parents by providing opportunity to realize that you can indeed work together when you share a singular goal: the children's development and well-being. This shift in mindset, focusing on shared purpose rather than personal grievance, can reduce the emotional reactivity that often escalates misunderstandings and fuels disputes. Instead of being triggered by the past, you become motivated by the present and future.

Not to be overlooked, effective coparenting can also benefit the parents. Where parents can communicate and work together for the benefit of the children, they can greatly reduce their own stress and the weight that is the natural outcome of parenting. We all know parenting is challenging at the best of times, and the added stresses of doing so while separated can make even small issues feel monumental.

Having a 'partner' through the journey of parenting can create a feeling of shared responsibility rather than feeling the load and burden which can make parents feel isolated and overwhelmed. The mutual support that comes from cooperative parenting not only lightens the load but also builds a rhythm that can benefit both homes by providing the space for parents to recover, recalibrate, and come back stronger. Shared problem-solving also models important life skills for children modelling conflict resolution, compromise, empathy, and resilience.

Key: I help you and you help me.

There is also something quietly reassuring about knowing that someone else is just as invested in your child's smile, their struggles, their milestones. It can feel like being part of a team again. That team does not have to resemble the one you imagined during your relationship, but when restructured with purpose and compassion, it can still be incredibly powerful. In some ways, it is a new kind of intimacy, not romantic, but rooted in respect and a common cause. It becomes about mutual trust and trusting that the other person is doing their best too, even if their way is different than yours. That sense of partnership, even if imperfect, brings clarity and hope to a complex dynamic.

Consequently, learning to establish a good coparenting relationship can help parents avoid very expensive and protracted legal battles. When parents are unable to settle into, at the very least, a civil coparenting relationship and are unable to communicate or cooperate, not only does the relationship steadily deteriorate but the result is often being left with no choice but to involve lawyers and sometimes the courts to resolve what could have been easily settled issues.

Litigation, or simply the involvement and expense of lawyers, is going to be emotionally and financially draining on both parents, and there is no avoiding this having a trickle-down impact on the children. The energy that could have been directed toward creating a peaceful home or planning for a child's future gets redirected to preparing for court appearances and funding legal fees. The atmosphere in both homes is absorbed by the children, you get to decide what that atmosphere is like.

When confronted with those occasions of needing to rely on professional help, it is always important to remember that you still lead the spirit of communication. Your words, your tone. What do you want to convey?

Taking the opportunity of learning how to communicate effectively with a coparent, sometimes the most negatively emotionally impactful relationship in our lives, can also have further-reaching benefits in establishing learned positive behaviours that can be applied in future relationships both personal and professional. Most importantly, every moment of choosing peace, of resisting the urge to retaliate, is a deposit into your child’s emotional bank account and sense of safety.

There is also a hidden gift in making peace with your coparent. Beyond the practicalities, it is an emotional unburdening, no longer giving your energy to resentment or old wounds. It is learning how to put down old swords, not because the pain wasn't real, but because peace serves your children better than war. And in choosing that, you may just begin to heal yourself, create space for new relationships, for deeper connections with your children, and for your own peace of mind.

Are there consequences to poor coparenting?

Poor coparenting can have serious negative effects on the lives and relationships of both parents and children.

Ineffective coparenting, however well-intended parents are, is going to have a negative and distressing impact on the children. When the parents are unable to cooperate and they engage in conflict, or refuse to work together, the children live in an environment charged with negativity and become conflicted, experience fear and anxiety. Often, when there is conflict, they will spend the time they have with one parent thinking about or concerned for the other. This can have a direct impact on the relationship between the child and the parent they are currently with.

After prolonged conflict between the parents, children may start to exhibit changes in behaviour and development both at school and in both homes. It is not uncommon for children to experience anxiety, loss of self-confidence, aggressiveness, and negatively distorted perceptions of relationships that they may carry into adulthood. They may internalize blame or adopt unhealthy coping strategies, believing that love and conflict are always intertwined.

Children learn how to love, how to disagree, and how to repair by watching the people closest to them. In the heat of parental conflict, their safe world begins to feel unpredictable. What they crave most is not luxury or entertainment, it is emotional security, and when that is threatened, everything else becomes harder: focusing on school, trusting adults, forming healthy friendships. Their entire world can tilt.

Aside from all the potential emotional landmines that a poor coparenting relationship may result in, there can be severe financial consequences when parents are not working together. If one parent begins to feel that they have tried enough, reached their limit of ability to communicate with the other parent, next steps can be to secure the assistance of a lawyer. Oftentimes, one letter sent from a lawyer can be enough of a wakeup call to settle the other side into a more amenable mood to take a step back and start over, but far too often that single letter can be the catalyst to costly litigation.

It is important to ensure that your lawyer does not send a letter that is overly aggressive or threatening. Instead, a letter that is firm and informative should be sufficient. It is crucial to keep in mind that while your lawyer is drafting the letter, and as I stated earlier in the chapter, you are the one who is ultimately responsible for its content since you were the one requesting it and it should reflect your thoughts. You will have the opportunity to review and authorize the letter before it is sent out, therefore, you cannot shift the blame to your lawyer if the letters tone causes negative consequences.

Key: You are in control of your legal process, do not relinquish that.

Litigation not only has an emotional impact on the children, but also on the parents, which can affect not just their own bottom line, but their current relationships, romantic or otherwise. It can distract them from the work that they do to earn money, cost them promotions, and possibly their jobs. It can leave them emotionally depleted and physically exhausted, limiting their ability to show up for their children in a meaningful way.

Protracted and acrimonious litigation is known to cause anxiety, depression, insomnia, and many other emotional strains and physical conditions. Even if a parent "wins" in court, the toll it takes often feels like a loss in many other areas.

Key: Put down your metaphorical weapons and stop looking at your coparent as an adversary.

Sometimes the bravest act is choosing not to react, not out of weakness, but out of wisdom. Choosing not to respond in anger, not to engage in petty tit-for-tat, has a quiet strength, a dignity, and when you choose that, again and again, you're modelling strength to your children. You are showing them that peace is power, and that they can rise above conflict instead of getting pulled under.

Coparenting is not about being perfect. It is about being present. It is about choosing your children's needs over your pride, your pain, or your need to be right. It is about understanding that your child's emotional safety is more important than your win in any argument. When you keep your focus on that, clarity follows.

It is about being present, patient, and predictable. Your child does not need you to be a superhero, they need you to be emotionally available, safe, and consistent.

Key: Post-divorce parenting begins with redefining your role and refocusing on your child's needs.

Reflection Prompt: Take a quiet moment to ask yourself: *What does my child need from me most right now?* The answer might be simpler than you think.

I remember thinking, "This can't possibly be this complicated." But it was, and it still is sometimes. If you feel that way too, you are not alone. Post-divorce parenting often starts with grief and confusion, but it grows into something steadier when you allow yourself to pause and lead with intention instead of reaction.

The foundation of your parenting is not built in courtrooms or through text message arguments. It is built in the quiet, repeated actions that show your children they are safe and loved, no matter what is happening between their parents.

Children do not need a perfect environment, they need a consistent one, and consistency can be your superpower.

Key: Consistency is the foundation of emotional security. Children thrive when they can predict what will happen next, even in the middle of transition.

If you have struggled to coparent well, you are not alone. Many people were not shown how to communicate in healthy ways or how to resolve conflict without escalation, but it is a skill that can be learned, and the more you practice it, the more empowered you become, not only as a parent, but as a human being.

Start with one thing, maybe it is a calmer response to a snippy message, maybe it is choosing to give the benefit of the doubt, or maybe it is letting go of something petty for the sake of something bigger. Start small, and let that momentum carry you.

In time, those small choices create big change, and that change, that steady shift toward peace and cooperation, is a legacy your children will carry with them far beyond childhood because in the end, coparenting is not about what happened between you, it is about what happens next for your children. It is not a rehashing of the past, but a reimagining of the future. You are no longer partners in life, but you are partners in something even more important: your child's well-being, identity, and future.

Coparenting is about showing up, even when it is hard. It is about taking a breath instead of taking a shot. It is about choosing maturity over mayhem, connection over control. It is about being the steady hand your child can rely on, the calm in the storm, the proof that love does not end just because a relationship does.

And when your children look back, what they will remember won't be the tension in the texts or the silence in the car, they will remember that somehow, even in the rubble of a broken relationship, you built something stable. They will remember that you both chose them again and again.

That is the legacy of coparenting done well: not perfection, but presence. Not agreement on every issue, but alignment on what matters most.

Because the truth is, your child does not need two perfect parents. They need two parents who keep trying.

Key: You do not have to agree on everything. You do have to agree that your child matters more than everything.

Let that be your legacy; raising peace, even when the past offered anything but.

Final Reflection Questions:

1. What emotions come up for you when you think about working with your coparent?

2. Are there specific triggers or patterns that consistently derail communication with your coparent? List 3 that come to mind.

3. Are there areas where you and your coparent already agree? How can you build on that common ground? List and explain.

4. What would it mean for your children if you and your coparent were truly cooperative? Name 3 areas they would feel benefit.

5. What would choosing peace look like in your next interaction with your coparent?

6. What do you want your children to say about how you handled coparenting?

7. What one step could you take this week that aligns with the coparenting relationship you want to build?

Your personal notes:

Chapter 2

Understanding the Impact of Divorce on Children

"Helping a child feel truly seen can sometimes heal wounds they do not yet have words for."

Divorce is an emotionally charged and life-altering experience for all members of a family, but children and young people experience it differently depending on their developmental stage. Understanding how children process divorce through the lens of their age helps us support them in ways that are compassionate, respectful, and effective. In this chapter, we explore the impacts of divorce across various age groups, highlighting their emotional, behavioural, and developmental needs, as well as providing strategies for support and healing.

Newborn to Age 4

Infants and toddlers are deeply impacted by divorce, even though they cannot express their emotions through language. Their primary need is for secure attachment, and any disruption in this bond whether, emotional or environmental, can feel confusing or even traumatic.

Babies and toddlers are sensitive to changes in routine, tone of voice, facial expressions, and the presence or absence of familiar caregivers. They pick up on tension even if they do not understand the words being said. Regressive behaviours, increased clinginess, feeding difficulties, or changes in sleep can signal distress.

Even when conflict is high or legal proceedings are underway, it is important to the baby's development to provide opportunities for frequent care by both parents. Their memories are short and limited and require frequent time with each parent to build a strong bond and sense of safety and security. Work with a professional if necessary to negotiate arrangements that will work with both of your schedules, and remember, everyone learns how to care for a baby for the first time at some point and basic care is something both parents are fully capable of providing.

Create consistency wherever possible. Maintain regular nap times, feeding schedules, and loving rituals like bedtime stories or lullabies. Use calming tones, slow transitions, and lots of physical closeness, holding, rocking, cuddling. Even if your toddler does not understand divorce, they do understand connection and comfort.

Key: Breastfeeding is a valid reason for infants to stay close to mom; it also requires special arrangements to include dad in the schedule.

Reflection Prompt: Consider your child's daily routine: are there moments where added reassurance or bonding could be offered?

Sometimes, small rituals, like a song before bed or a gentle morning hug, can be anchors in a sea of change. In the absence of genuine safety concerns, do everything possible not to place unnecessary obstacles in the path of your baby's growth by impeding a strong and healthy bond with their other parent.

Children Ages 4–12

Divorce can feel earth-shattering to children in this age group. Their world is primarily defined by the love and security of their parents, so a significant change in that foundation may leave them feeling confused, scared, and deeply unsettled.

They may not have the words to express how they are feeling, and without support, those big emotions can show up as tantrums, withdrawal, regressions, or even physical complaints like stomach aches.

If their comments or answers seem unexpected or off-topic, they may not understand the thought or the question, or they may simply need more time to form their thoughts. Be patient and offer reassurance through your tone and body language.

Often, children at this stage believe the divorce is their fault, leading to unnecessary guilt and shame.

Emotional Impacts

Children may experience a whirlwind of emotions including anger, sadness, confusion, and anxiety. Self-blame is common, as they try to make sense of the changes around them.

Strategy

Create a nurturing environment where your child feels emotionally safe. Reassure them frequently that the divorce is not their fault. Validate their feelings, even if their feelings do not seem to 'make sense' to you, and help them name and explore what they are feeling.

Coping Methods for Children

- Expressing their feelings: Art, drawing, storytelling, or play can be powerful tools to help children work through emotions.
- Maintaining routines: Familiar routines help children feel secure in times of change.
- Seeking support: Enlist trusted adults like grandparents, teachers, or counsellors, to reinforce emotional safety.
- Staying active: Physical movement can help children release stress and pent-up energy.
- Focusing on positives: Help your child find joy in hobbies, friendships, and interests.
- Learning new skills: New activities build confidence and remind children that growth is possible.

Communication Tips: Ages 4–7

Young children need concrete, specific communication. Use names, not pronouns, and avoid vague time references. Instead of "What happened yesterday?" ask, "What did you do after breakfast?" Avoid asking, "How did that make you feel?" Instead, try, "Did you feel scared?" or "What part of that made you sad?" Be cautious not to assume or give them thoughts and/or emotions.

If their answers seem unexpected or off-topic, they may not understand the question. Always check for understanding gently.

Anecdote

A Personal Story

My current husband's daughter was 5 when we became a family. He had just exited a long-term relationship with the only partner his daughter knew other than her mother. She also had a stepfather and baby brother in her home with her mom.

I became concerned about a "sore leg" that she complained about quite often, asking her dad to carry her when we were out, or needing it attended to when we were home.

During a phone call with her mother, I gently asked about their daughter's sore leg and was there anything I needed to do or could help with. Mom assured me she was aware of the sore leg and was looking into a chiropractic appointment.

After a few more weekends watching the "sore leg" come and go, receive no treatment, and many conversations with her, I decided to gently explore what I sensed might be an emotional need in disguise.

I asked, "...you know how you get a sore leg all the time, is your leg really sore in your leg, or is your leg sore up here?" as I put my hand on her chest. She tilted her head and smiled, asking "How did you know?"

I told her, "I've been a mommy for a really long time, I've seen sore legs come and I've seen sore legs go and sometimes I know that sore legs can actually be sore somewhere else and that's okay. But I want you to know that if you need a hug, or if you need some attention or just to know that we love you, you just have to let us know, because we all love you very much."

She moved in for a big hug. We never heard about a sore leg again. When she wanted to be carried, she asked to be carried. If she wanted attention, she asked for playtime.

Sometimes, what children need most is not a solution, it is to be seen, heard, and loved.

Communication Tips: Ages 8–12

While this group may sound more articulate, their logic and memory are still developing. They may appear to understand more than they actually do. Stick with concrete questions, avoid assumptions, and ask for clarification. Be patient. This is a time when they need consistency, clear roles, and firm but loving guidance.

Reflection Prompt: Think about a time when your child seemed overwhelmed or confused. How did you respond? What might you do differently now, knowing what you know about their developmental needs?

Adolescents (13+)

Adolescents are already in the thick of identity exploration, social pressure, and emotional ups and downs. Add divorce to the mix, and things can become volatile or overwhelming. They may feel caught in the middle, pressured to choose sides, or resentful about having no say in the matter. Yet they may also hide their feelings, presenting a stoic or detached front.

Conflicted Loyalties

Teens often feel like they must take sides, especially when parents speak negatively about each other.

Even as they push you away or seem indifferent, adolescents still deeply crave security, understanding, and acceptance from their parents.

Strategy

Reassure them that it is not their job to choose. Actively discourage side-taking and emphasize that they are allowed, and encouraged, to love both parents.

Emotional Impacts

Teens may cycle through intense emotions including anger, fear, anxiety, and even numbness.

Strategy

Listen without judgment. Let them know protecting you is not their responsibility. Let your home be a safe haven, not another battleground.

Relationship Impacts

Your adolescent may pull away from one or both parents as they try to make sense of the changes.

Strategy

Encourage connection without pressure. Respect their autonomy but continue to show up consistently and lovingly.

Behavioural Impacts

Teens may withdraw, become irritable, struggle in school, or act out in risky ways.

Strategy

Keep routines predictable. Involve school personnel if needed and seek outside support when behaviours become concerning.

Coping Methods for Adolescents

- Creative outlets: Writing, art, and music help teens express what words can't.
- Support networks: Encourage friendships and mentor relationships with caring, trusted adults.
- Healthy routines: Sleep, food, and movement regulate emotions.
- Goal setting: Encourages forward thinking and optimism.
- Volunteering or hobbies: Builds self-esteem and offers distraction from stress.
- Counselling: Provides a private space to process change.

Communication Tips for Adolescents

Teens often want more information but will not yet have the life experience to process it all. Keep communication age-appropriate and need-to-know. Use clear, positive language and avoid sarcasm or emotional dumping.

Reflection Prompt: Have you ever found yourself confiding too much in your teen? Reflect on how you can create boundaries that respect their need for safety, not secrets.

Young Adults (18+ and beyond)

Many parents assume that because their children are legally adults, they are emotionally immune to divorce. This is far from true. Young adults may experience identity confusion, grief, and even fear about their own future relationships.

Identity Impacts

Young adults may reevaluate everything they thought they knew about love, commitment, and family.

Strategy

Encourage exploration. Reassure them that they are not doomed to repeat the past. Help them find therapeutic support if needed.

Relationship Impacts

Relationships with one or both parents may shift.

Strategy

Avoid making your adult child your confidant. Let them be your child, not your therapist.

Emotional Impacts

They may feel betrayed, anxious, or sad, especially if the divorce seems sudden.

Strategy

Avoid getting defensive. Let them speak their truth and offer a listening ear, not solutions.

Financial Impacts

Young adults may face unexpected financial strain during your divorce.

Strategy

Be honest about what you can offer and help them plan accordingly.

Coping Methods for Young Adults

- Building community: Friendships and mentorships create grounding.
- Practicing self-care: Encourages healing and balance.
- Exploring identity: Finding meaning in hobbies or career goals.
- Mindfulness: Encourages resilience through inner awareness.
- Professional support: Therapy provides space to integrate change.

Communication Tips for Young Adults

Be the parent, not the best friend, not the wounded party. They are still not your emotional caretaker.

Reflection Prompt: Are you unintentionally using your adult child for support in ways that belong with a peer or professional? How can you gently return to being a grounded, supportive parent?

Conclusion

No matter their age, children need stability, love, and reassurance when their family dynamic shifts. Divorce may look different at 4, 14, or 24, but the common thread is the need for safe, supportive relationships with both parents. When parents prioritize their children's well-being over their own hurt, healing becomes possible.

Key: Regardless of age, children who are experiencing the separation or divorce of their parents need support from both parents and both sides of their family whether you like them or not.

Putting your children first is a beautiful principle, and an incredibly difficult practice. It requires setting aside ego, managing emotion, and sometimes choosing the higher road when you are exhausted and frustrated.

Key: Putting children first means protecting their emotional well-being, even when it might be inconvenient or unfair to you.

Reflection Prompt: Ask yourself, "Am I responding in a way that supports my child's peace, or my own frustration?" Both are valid, but awareness matters.

There were days when I had to remind myself, sometimes out loud, that putting my child first did not mean pretending I wasn't hurting. It just meant I had to pause, breathe, and choose differently. That pause, that breath, it became the space where I started to parent differently. Not perfectly, just more consciously.

Children are highly sensitive to tension and even when you think you are keeping the conflict quiet, they feel it in their bodies. Putting them first does not mean pretending everything is perfect, it means shielding them from being dragged into battles they did not choose.

You may not be able to control what happens at the other home, but you can shape the emotional tone of your own. You can offer calm when chaos shows up at the door. You can provide truth without venom, honesty without blame.

One parent recently said to me, "I don't know if I can restrain myself."

I responded, "It isn't about restraint, it is about love."

Key: Every moment you stay grounded becomes a thread of safety your child can hold onto.

No parent handles this journey perfectly but showing up with love, patience, and presence makes all the difference.

Final Reflection Questions

1. **Which stage of your child's development are you navigating right now? How are they showing you what they need?**

2. **Are there routines or rituals you could strengthen to offer stability and comfort? Name 3 and explain.**

3. **How do you communicate differently with your children based on their age? What might you adjust?**

4. **Have you found yourself relying emotionally on your children, young or adult, in ways that might burden them? How can you create healthier support systems?**

5. **What is one simple action you can take this week to deepen your child's sense of safety, love, and belonging?**

Your personal Notes:

Chapter 3

Explaining the Divorce to Your Children

"In the storm of change, you are their anchor. With each act of patience, grace, and steady love, you help them believe that even when families shift, love remains."

Telling your children about your separation is one of the most delicate and important conversations you will ever have. It is a moment that has the power to shape how your children move through the process of your separation, adjust to life after divorce, and even how they approach relationships in adulthood. This chapter is about helping you approach that moment with care, compassion, and confidence.

This will likely be one of the hardest conversations you will ever have as a parent, and one of the most meaningful. It is okay to feel anxious, sad, or unsure. What matters most is showing up with honesty and love.

There is no perfect time to have this conversation, but there are better times, moments when emotions are relatively stable, when both parents can be present, and when there is enough time to offer your children the comfort and space they will need. One thing is certain: this is a conversation that deserves to be taken very seriously.

Why Both Parents Should Be Present

Whenever possible, both parents should be present when telling the children about the separation. This unified approach sends a clear message: the decision to separate is mutual, and both parents still love their children deeply and will continue to be there for them. Children are incredibly perceptive and will take cues not just from your words, but from your tone, your body language, and whether you can sit together without conflict.

Reflection Prompt: Can you and your coparent sit together calmly for this conversation? If not, what steps can you take to prepare yourself emotionally?

If you feel unable to manage this conversation appropriately, whether due to anger, grief, or high conflict, consider seeking short-term counselling or mediation to help you prepare. Your emotional readiness is just as important as the script you choose.

A Script That Works

Over the years, I have helped many parents deliver this message using a carefully crafted script that has consistently led to the most positive outcomes. Let's break it down into three essential parts:

Part One:

"Mom and Dad have decided together that even though we love each other, we don't love each other in the way you do when you live together as a couple."

This line accomplishes two critical things:

- It emphasizes that the decision was made *together*, preventing children from assigning blame.
- It acknowledges that there is still love between the parents, which reassures children who might fear that love can simply disappear.

Children may wonder: *If my parents can stop loving each other, could they stop loving me too?* Reassuring them that your love for them is constant and unchanging is key.

Younger children may need simpler language and more concrete reassurances about day-to-day life, while older children might ask harder questions or want to understand more about why this is happening. Tailor your words to their developmental stage while keeping the core message the same: this is not their fault, and they are deeply loved.

Key: Children need frequent, clear reminders that your love for them will never fade.

Reflection Prompt: How might your children interpret your separation if you cannot clarify that love still exists between both parents and them?

Part Two:

"Dad knows how much you love mom, and how very much mom loves you. That makes me very happy, and it's very important to me."

This sentence should be echoed by the other parent immediately after. This simple, powerful statement gives your children *permission* to love both parents openly, without guilt or fear of upsetting one of you.

When you have said these words, you are making a promise. Later, when your children talk about their other parent, even if it is hard for you to hear, you must honour that promise. Children should never feel like they must hide a part of their life from you.

Remember, if a child does not feel safe or comfortable talking to you about the positives in their other home, will they feel safe and comfortable telling you about the scary or negative things that may be happening?

Key: Children need to feel safe talking about their other parent with you.

Reflection Prompt: Have you ever unintentionally discouraged your children from talking about your coparent? How can you change that?

Part Three:

"We want you to know that even though we will no longer live in the same house, we are both still your parents and will be talking about you all the time. We will continue to work together as a team to make decisions about you. We both love you very much, and that will never change."

This reassures children that some things will change, but not everything. They are still loved, supported, and seen by both parents. This third part of the script also gives children a sense of what comes next, even if you do not have all the answers yet.

Avoid the temptation to explain the reasons for your divorce in too much detail. Children do not need to know about infidelity, financial struggles, or emotional disconnects, they need to know they are safe, loved, and not to blame.

Key: Parents who communicate and work together provide security for their children.

Navigating the Questions

After the initial conversation, your children may have many questions. Where will they live? Will they have to move? Will they still see their friends? It is okay not to have all the answers. Be honest, be age-appropriate, and never make promises you are unsure you can keep. Try not to assume that you will buy the other parent out or keep the family home. As the process unfolds, you may learn more about your finances and emotional needs, which can change the outcome.

A helpful response might be:

"We're still working out the details, but we promise to keep you updated as soon as we know more."

This communicates respect, responsibility, and care and when it comes to uncertain things, like whether the family home will be sold, be cautious. If plans change, children may feel betrayed if you made

premature promises.

On friendships:

"Of course, you'll still see your friends. We'll make sure you can keep those important relationships."

Reflection Prompt: What promises are you tempted to make right now? Are they ones you can truly keep?

Modelling Positive Coparenting

This first conversation sets the tone. Children need to see that their parents can still communicate, even if things are hard. If possible, remain available for a few hours after the conversation. If one parent leaves too quickly, children might assume they are the one to blame or believe one parent was 'kicked out.'

And what if only one parent delivers the news?

Sometimes, the ideal situation is not possible. If only one parent is able or willing to speak with the children, it becomes even more important to stay neutral. If you find yourself in this situation, consider involving a neutral third party such as a professional or family member of the other parent. They can help you stay focused on your child's needs instead of your own pain or anger.

Key Takeaway: Focus on your children's emotional safety by setting aside blame, even when it is hard.

It is paramount that you do not assign blame, even subtly, it damages trust. Saying things like, "Your (other parent) is a deadbeat," or "Your (other parent) looks like a sloth" with contempt can hurt deeply. Children identify with both parents. If you show disdain for your coparent, they may internalize that as self-rejection. When they hear how much they are like that parent, in a genuinely positive way, will they be able to happily accept it, or do they fear you see them the way you describe that parent?

Reflection Prompt: How can you avoid even subtle negativity when speaking about your coparent?

Anecdote

A Personal Story

To show you just how important this conversation can be, I want to share a deeply personal story from my own life.

Looking way back to 1995, I wish someone had guided me through this. I know firsthand how important it could have been for my children to have had both of us present when they were told.

The day after discovering my husband's affair, without giving them the details, I told my children, that their father had moved out and was now living at grandmas.

My son was not surprised; he already knew about the relationship and told me he knew it was because his dad had a girlfriend, this is when he shared that he refused to attend when they took a day trip to the zoo. My daughter, eight at the time, mentioned a sleepover that involved the girlfriend. I tried to stay composed, but I was heartbroken, and my children could tell. They tried to comfort me. They told me they loved me. But that was not their job.

If my coparent and I had talked first, if we had prepared, we could have shared the news together, calmly and lovingly. There was information that he knew the children had, that I did not, and knowing that information could have significantly changed my immediate reaction to hearing those stories from my children. I hope he would have been honest about involving the children, but I regret not having given them the chance to hear it from both of us together.

Reflection Activity: Write an anecdote of your own:

- Describe a time when coparenting communication failed.
- How did it affect your children?
- How could you have handled it better?
- How could your coparent have handled it better?

Your children are not responsible for your pain, your anger, or your heartbreak. They need you to be steady, kind, and clear. You may not have chosen divorce, but you can choose how you handle it, and that choice can make all the difference for your children's healing and growth.

This may feel like the end of a family, but it can be the beginning of a new way of loving and parenting your children. With care and intention, your children can thrive, not in spite of the divorce, but because you handled it with grace, honesty, and love.

Final Reflection Questions

1. **How do you want your children to remember this conversation?**

2. **What emotions do you want to leave them with?**

3. **How can you and your coparent prepare together, even if your relationship is strained?**

4. **What consistent messages can you give your children over the next year to reinforce their sense of security?**

Your Personal Notes:

Chapter 4

The Vital Importance of Following Your Parenting Plan

"A parenting plan is not just a legal formality, it is a promise of reliability. It tells your child: You can count on us, even when everything else feels uncertain."

Now that the children know, what is parenting going to look like?

In an ideal world, every parenting plan would be created with thoughtfulness, mutual respect, and a genuine focus on the children's well-being. It would reflect the unique rhythms of the family, consider each parent's strengths, and most importantly, offer children the structure and emotional safety they need to thrive. But the reality is not always so graceful. Many parents are left without a clear plan, or they find themselves bound to one that was handed down by a court, often with little room for the family's real-life dynamics. Others accept plans crafted in legal negotiations, shaped more by strategy than by the heart of parenting.

When there is no plan, or when the one in place does not truly fit, it is like sailing without a compass. Parents may be unsure of what to expect from each other, and children often feel that uncertainty most. Routines become unpredictable, boundaries blur, and tensions rise. And while the adults may be coping in their own ways, children can internalize that instability in ways we may not always see right away. They need to know where they will sleep, who will pick them up, and whether they will be at Grandma's house for Sunday dinner. Predictability is not just a convenience, it is comfort. It is the soil in which their emotional security grows.

Regrettably, many parents lack a comprehensive parenting plan or are subject to a court-ordered plan that may have significant gaps. Others may rely on a plan developed by lawyers that prioritizes the parents' wishes rather than the children's best interests.

The consequences of not having a parenting plan can be significant and potentially harmful for both the parents and the children. Without a clear and comprehensive plan in place, parents may struggle to establish clear expectations and boundaries for their children. This leads to a period of confusion and conflict.

A lack of structure can also cause disruptions to the children's routines and sense of stability, which can impact their emotional well-being and overall development.

Reflection Prompt: Think back to a moment when the parenting plan wasn't clear, or maybe there was no plan at all. How did you feel? How did your children seem to respond? What might have been different if a clear path had been in place?

In the absence of a parenting plan, parents may also find it difficult to make important decisions about their children's education, health care, and other important aspects of not only the children's lives, but their own lives as well.

In the worst-case scenario, the lack of a parenting plan may lead to prolonged legal battles and disputes, which can be emotionally and financially draining for everyone.

Key: Having a parenting plan provides everyone with a clear schedule they can rely upon.

Having a court-ordered parenting plan that neither parent aligns with can also have negative consequences. When the plan feels like something forced on you, not something created with you, it can be hard to follow with your full conviction. Although a court-ordered plan is designed to provide structure and guidelines for coparenting, it may not always address the unique needs and circumstances of the parents and children involved. As a result, one or both parents may feel frustrated or dissatisfied with the plan and may be less likely to comply with its terms. This can lead to ongoing conflicts, disputes, and an overall breakdown in communication between the parents.

Children may also be negatively affected by the tension and animosity between their parents, which can impact their mental and emotional well-being. In some cases, a court-ordered plan may also fail to address significant issues or changes that arise after the plan is put in place, which can create additional stress and difficulties for the parents and children.

Key: Parents are far more likely to comply with the terms of a parenting plan they agreed upon rather than one that has been imposed on them.

A parenting plan that is developed between lawyers and takes only the parents' demands into consideration can also have negative consequences. In such a situation, the needs and best interests of the children may be overlooked or given less priority, which can lead to an unbalanced and unfair plan.

Additionally, such a plan may not consider the unique circumstances and dynamics of the family, which can result in a plan that does not work well for the children or the parents.

I have also found that parents sometimes acquiesce to things they do not necessarily want in a parenting plan when litigating because they are exhausted, financially drained, or as a trade-off for something else in the financial or property settlement that does not relate to the children. This is not putting the children's needs and best interests first.

It is also important to understand that if you make a promise during litigation to gain a desired outcome or to persuade the court, and that promise is not explicitly written into the final parenting plan, you are still morally and ethically obligated to follow through. If you received the thing you wanted based on your word, even if it did not end up in writing, keeping that promise reflects integrity and reinforces trust in your coparenting relationship. Children benefit when parents model accountability. However, get it in writing.

Similarly, if you make a commitment or offer within your litigation pleadings, perhaps as a rationale for a particular arrangement or to persuade the court to adopt your preferred outcome, and the parenting plan ultimately reflects your desired outcome but does not formally include your offer or promise, you are still responsible for upholding what you said. Following through on those representations, even if not written into the plan, demonstrates your integrity, respect for the legal process, and willingness to parent in good faith. This level of consistency and reliability ultimately benefits your child.

Reflection Prompt: Did you make any verbal assurances, offers, or statements during the legal process to get something you wanted, perhaps more parenting time, or a particular decision-making responsibility?

Even if those words did not end up in the final written plan, do you believe your child would benefit from you honouring that commitment anyway? Modelling this kind of integrity not only builds trust with your coparent but strengthens your role as a guide for your child's developing values.

When a parenting plan does not reflect your children's real needs, or the true shape of your family, it can invite ongoing conflict and tension between parents.

Children often absorb this conflict more deeply than we realize. They may experience anxiety, stress, or a general sense of confusion about where they belong and who they can depend on.

Moreover, a plan that does not address the children's needs may fail to provide them with a stable and predictable routine, which can make it difficult for them to adjust to the changes that come with a divorce or separation.

It is natural to feel guilty after a separation or to hope that small gestures like giving in on a parenting time detail or making extra accommodations might soften the other parent or create a friendlier dynamic, but giving in out of guilt or in hopes of getting something back, whether it is flexibility, appreciation, or even friendship, often backfires. When those hopes are not met and that guilt turns into regret, resentment can build quickly. Resentment erodes your well-being and can strain your parenting. It is healthier to make decisions based on what is right and sustainable, not on guilt or wishful thinking.

Overall, it is important for parents to prioritize the needs of their children when developing a parenting plan and to work together to create a plan that is fair, balanced, and in the best interests of the children.

Key: A parenting plan that is developed with the input of both parents is more likely to succeed and will help reduce potential future conflict.

Following a parenting plan is crucial for coparenting success. A parenting plan is an agreement that outlines the terms of parenting time and decision-making for the children of divorced or separated parents.

The plan is designed to ensure that both parents have a clear understanding of their rights and responsibilities, as well as the expectations for how the children will be cared for and raised.

For the Children

By following a parenting plan, parents can avoid misunderstandings and conflicts that can arise from inconsistent or unclear communication. This can help to create a stable and predictable environment for the children, which is essential for their emotional well-being and development.

Following a parenting plan can also help to minimize the stress and disruption that can occur for the children during the transition to a new family dynamic.

Finally, following a parenting plan demonstrates to the children that both parents are committed to their well-being and are working together to provide for their needs. This can help to create a sense of security and stability for the children, which is essential for their healthy development.

When parents follow a parenting plan, they are not only ensuring that their children's needs are being met, but they are also demonstrating to the children that they are willing to work together for their benefit. This can go a long way in establishing a positive coparenting relationship, even if the parents cannot always see eye to eye.

One of the benefits of following a parenting plan is that it provides a clear and consistent structure for the children's lives. Children thrive on routine and predictability, and a well-crafted parenting plan can provide just that.

For the Parents

The parenting plan sets out clear guidelines for when each parent will have parenting time with the children, how decisions will be made regarding the children's upbringing, and how conflicts will be resolved. This can help to minimize the potential for confusion, misunderstandings, and disagreements, which can ultimately benefit both the children and their parents.

Following a parenting plan can also help to establish boundaries and expectations between the parents. By agreeing to a set of guidelines for coparenting, each parent knows what is expected of them and what they can expect from the other parent. This can help reduce the likelihood of disputes and make it easier for the parents to work together effectively.

It provides the parents with the confidence to manage other aspects of their lives, knowing there is a set schedule to rely on.

At its best, a parenting plan is not a legal document, it is a lifeline. A bridge between homes. Consistency.

Key: Following a parenting plan can help to minimize the impact of the divorce or separation on the children by providing security and consistency.

Children can experience a wide range of emotions when their parents separate, including confusion, fear, anger, and sadness. By providing a stable and predictable environment, a parenting plan can help to ease these feelings.

Reflection Prompt: Think about how your children respond to structure. Have you noticed a change in their behaviour or mood when routines are disrupted? How can consistency support their sense of safety?

While it is important to have a parenting plan in place to provide structure and consistency, it is also important to be flexible when necessary for the benefit of the children.

Children's needs and schedules can change over time, and it is important for parents to be able to adapt the parenting plan accordingly. For example, if one of the children has a new extracurricular activity that they are passionate about, the parenting plan may need to be adjusted to accommodate that activity. Similarly, if one parent's work schedule changes, the parenting plan may need to be adjusted to ensure that the children's needs are still being met.

It is crucial for parents to recognize that special occasions may occur on the other parent's scheduled parenting time and that it is vital for the children to participate in those celebrations to prevent them from feeling left out. Parents must be adaptable in permitting them to attend such events as they may feel excluded presently or in the future when they notice their absence in family photos or conversations. It helps when parents can be flexible, making room for children to feel part of the families they love.

Although some parents may prefer to assume that their children won't feel left out if the other parent does not discuss the event with them, it is essential to remember that we cannot regulate what they hear from other people, especially other children.

Being flexible in the parenting plan can also help to build trust and foster a positive coparenting relationship. If one parent is willing to be accommodating and make changes, when necessary, it can demonstrate to the other parent that they are committed to working together for the benefit of the children. This can help to reduce the potential for conflicts and improve communication between the parents.

Reflection Prompt: When have you been flexible with your coparent for your child's benefit? What was the outcome and how did your child feel?

However, it is important to note that any changes to the parenting plan should be made in accordance with the best interest of the children in mind. Both parents should be involved in the decision-making process and should agree to any changes before they are made.

Whenever parents agree to a flexible change in the parenting plan, they should ensure that it is documented in writing, via a communications app or e-mail, with all details confirmed. This helps to avoid any misunderstandings or disputes that may arise in the future. There are several apps to choose from; consult your lawyer or family dispute specialist for the app best suited to your family's needs.

Parenting plans exist for a reason: to provide predictability and reduce conflict. But let's be honest, there are days when sticking to the plan feels like climbing uphill in a storm. Plans get ignored, pushed, challenged. Sometimes by the other parent, sometimes by life itself.

Key: The parenting plan is not about control. It is about clarity. It gives children a sense of security in an otherwise unstable situation.

Reflection Prompt: Ask yourself, "Am I using the plan to create peace, or to win?" When used right, it is a safety net and not a weapon.

I can't tell you how many times the other parent tried to pull me off course, and sometimes it worked, but over time I learned consistency is the quiet power move. You do not have to explain yourself over and over.

You should not engage in every emotional tug-of-war, you just return to the plan, gently but firmly.

And when the plan does not work? You revise it with the child in mind, not the conflict. Sometimes coparents treat parenting plans like a scoreboard, but your child is not keeping score, they are watching for steadiness, they are feeling for safety.

You may not always feel appreciated in the moment, but trust that every time you honour the plan, you are giving your child one more reason to exhale.

Key: Predictability is an invisible gift. It tells your child: "No matter what's happening, you can count on me."

My recommendation for those who do not use a communication app is to create a designated e-mail folder titled something like "Parenting Comms" or a name that suits your preference. Avoid derogatory terms that your children may come across. Whenever you send an e-mail, save it to this folder. In cases where you reach a mutual agreement on schedule flexibility, send an e-mail to the other parent outlining all the details, such as:

"We agreed today that I'll pick up the kids on Saturday, February 23rd, 2029, at 2:00 PM instead of the scheduled 5:00 PM, to take them to my parents' anniversary dinner. Please confirm."

The other parent should reply with a simple "confirmed," and you should save this e-mail to your communication folder.

I understand that some parents may find the practice of documenting changes in the parenting plan to be tedious, however, it is essential to do so as it helps to avoid potential conflicts that may arise due to misunderstandings or disagreements.

It is important to remember that in some cases, the other parent may forget about the changes they have agreed to, while in other cases, they may willfully refuse to follow through on the agreed-upon changes. This may be a result of a personal schedule change or possibly issues that have arisen in the coparenting relationship between the time of the agreement and the date of the event which have not yet been resolved.

In either case, having documented proof of the agreement, such as an e-mail, can help to remind the forgetful parent and hold the unwilling parent accountable for their actions or lack thereof.

Furthermore, having a written record of the agreement can help to resolve any disputes that may arise and can serve as proof if the issue needs to be escalated to legal or mediation process. This can be especially helpful in situations where the coparenting relationship has broken down and both parents are struggling to communicate effectively. By having a written record of the agreement, both parties can refer to it and ensure that they are adhering to the agreed-upon terms.

Key: A clear parenting plan is essential, but so is the flexibility to meet your children's evolving needs. It is important to keep in mind that while we consider it our time, it is the children's time, and their enjoyment of that time should be a top priority.

A clear, detailed parenting plan isn't just paperwork, it is your child's safety net. When storms come, and emotions run high, that written agreement becomes a quiet anchor, reminding everyone where home base is.

Considering it the minimum agreement that both parents are willing to live with if they are not getting along, it can provide a framework for making decisions that prioritize the children's well-being, which can change from time to time while trying to negotiate a variable option.

Ultimately, both parents should strive to be flexible and cooperative while also maintaining their commitment to the well-being of their children.

It is important to keep in mind that refusing a reasonable request for flexibility can lead to a tit-for-tat dynamic that creates unnecessary drama and conflict. This can ultimately harm the children by preventing them from participating in important events with both sides of the family.

Key: The parenting plan should be considered your fallback plan, the minimum you are willing to live with when you are not getting along.

If one parent unreasonably refuses a request for flexibility, it is likely that the other parent will remember this in the future and be less willing to accommodate similar requests. It is essential to work together and find a way to be flexible and cooperative, even in situations where it may be difficult or inconvenient.

By putting the children's needs first and working together to find solutions that benefit everyone involved, both parents can avoid the negative consequences of a spiteful tit-for-tat dynamic. This can help to create a more positive coparenting relationship that prioritizes the well-being and happiness of the children.

Anecdote

Professional Story

What I see far too often, as with one family in particular, attempts were made to coparent without a parenting plan, eventually leading to more difficult negotiations when they attended for mediation.

Initially, things were going smoothly when there were no external factors hindering their ability to cooperate. However, as time passed and circumstances changed, such as new partners, growing distance between parents, or changing dynamics, cooperation became more challenging.

This led to conflict, which made it more difficult for them to reach an agreement, particularly when one or both parties have become entrenched on issues that were not problematic initially.

This grew from the mounting animosity, influence from a new partner, and the new partner's parenting plan with their own children.

If they had sought mediation or created a thorough parenting plan in the early stages of their separation, it would have saved them a significant amount of time, money, and stress.

Reflection Prompt: Write an anecdote of your own describing how not following the parenting plan created a problem. How did it affect the children? How could you have handled it better? How could your coparent have handled it better?

Closing Thought: A strong parenting plan is not about rules and rigidity, it is about building a foundation your children can count on. The plan is your map, but the heart behind it is what brings the journey to life. When both parents show up with commitment, cooperation, and compassion, they create something far more powerful than a schedule, they create peace, predictability, and love that children will carry with them for years to come. You will find a sample parenting plan at the end of Ch. 16.

Final Reflection Questions:

1. **What is one specific aspect of your current parenting plan that's working well? How can you build on that success?**

2. **Are there any parts of your plan that consistently cause tension or confusion? What might need to be adjusted?**

3. **Have you and your coparent talked about the plan recently? If not, how might revisiting it together benefit your children?**

4. **How do you typically respond when flexibility is needed? Is there room to be more understanding, or more clear?**

5. **What message do you want your children to receive when they observe how you and their other parent handle requests for flexibility in the parenting plan?**

Your Personal Notes:

Chapter 5

The Importance of Not Involving Children in the Parenting Time Conversations

Divorce and separation are challenging for everyone, and as parents, we want to make sure our children are supported throughout the transition. With this in mind, it is crucial that we never ask our children to choose between their parents or to take sides in decisions about where they will live. The emotional weight of such a decision can be overwhelming, and it puts an undue burden on children. Asking them to make such a monumental choice can cause stress, confusion, and feelings of guilt that can last long after the decision is made.

Children are often not equipped to fully understand the implications of these decisions, nor should they have to shoulder that responsibility. This is why it is so important to avoid canvassing children about who they want to live with. While it may seem like a natural question to ask, it places children in a difficult position. They may feel they need to choose one parent over the other, or worse, they may feel responsible for the breakup of the family. This emotional confusion can be lasting and deep.

It is profoundly difficult to watch your child struggle, and it is natural to want to fix it by giving them more control. However, sometimes, protecting their innocence means holding that boundary.

Furthermore, when children are asked to choose which parent they want to live with, it can create an unhealthy power dynamic. The child may feel they need to "please" one parent, or that they must say what the parent wants to hear, rather than expressing their own feelings. This can ultimately lead to emotional manipulation, whether intentional or not.

Key: Children are not equipped to make decisions about parenting time arrangements.

It is not unusual for children to sometimes feel closer to one parent or the other, and if asked about their preference, this can place them in an emotionally fraught situation. They might feel guilt, disloyalty, or even shame for having a preference at all, because they still love equally.

This internal turmoil is confusing for children, especially when they do not have the maturity or understanding to navigate the complexities of the situation. They may feel torn, which can lead them to distance themselves emotionally from one or both parents.

One of the most damaging aspects of involving children in the decision about where they want to live is the risk of inadvertently causing emotional distancing from one of the parents. If a child feels manipulated by a parent, they may try to distance themselves emotionally to avoid feelings of guilt or disloyalty. This can create a divide between the parent and child that might be difficult to repair, further complicating the situation for everyone.

Reflection Prompt: Can you recall a moment when your child expressed a preference for one parent over the other? How did you respond, and how do you think that impacted your child's feelings toward the other parent?

It is vital for parents to remember that children's complaints about the other parent, while common, do not necessarily signal a desire to change the parenting plan or the living arrangement. Children often complain about the other parent due to simple, age-appropriate struggles, like missing their friends, homesickness, or typical parent-child conflicts. These complaints are often temporary and should not be treated as a reason to make drastic changes to the custody schedule.

It is essential for parents to listen to their child's concerns with empathy, but without using these complaints as an opportunity to manipulate the child into taking sides. By listening and offering support, rather than attempting to pursue an agenda, parents can help children feel heard and understood. It is important to avoid negative talk about the other parent, even when emotions are running high. Children need a safe space where they can express their feelings without fear of judgment or manipulation.

Key: Including children in the decision-making process could cause them to distance themselves emotionally from one parent or both.

When parents engage in the manipulation of their child's feelings, it can result in the child feeling torn between parents. They may feel as though their love for one parent is in conflict with their love for the other, creating unnecessary emotional stress leading to resentment and disengagement.

Instead of involving children in these decisions, parents should strive to create a coparenting relationship that places the child's well-being first. This means avoiding speaking negatively about the other parent, working to maintain a positive and respectful relationship, and, when necessary, seeking outside support, whether through therapy, counselling, or mediation, to help navigate the complexities of the relationship.

It is also important to note that, unfortunately, some parents may enter coparenting with the intention of controlling the other parent or limiting their time with the children. This approach is deeply harmful to the children, and it often leads to emotional crises and damaged relationships. Coparenting should never be used as a way to "win" or gain control; instead, it should be an effort to cooperate and create a healthy environment for the children.

Reflection Prompt: Have you ever struggled with feeling that your coparent is trying to manipulate the situation? How did you handle it, and what do you think the impact was on your child?

When coparenting dynamics become difficult, it can be helpful to seek counselling or mediation to address these issues. These resources can provide a neutral space for both parents to discuss their concerns and find more productive ways to coparent in the best interest of the children.

Validating your child's feelings is incredibly important. If a child expresses discomfort or a concern about the other parent's home, the response should be one of empathy and understanding. It is essential that parents avoid exaggerating or making the issue seem bigger than it is.

Conversely, minimizing or dismissing a child's concerns can make them feel as though their emotions are invalid, which only contributes to insecurity and confusion.

It is also important to remember that the child's perspective is their reality. What may seem like a small issue to you could be a significant concern for them. Listening to and understanding their feelings can help them feel supported.

Key: Never manipulate your child into embellishing their complaints, as it risks them not sharing any real concerns in the future.

Parents must approach these situations with patience and empathy, listening without judgment. If the child's complaint is valid, work together with the coparent to find a solution that addresses their concern. Avoid taking sides or making one parent's house seem "better" than the other. Instead, encourage open communication and work to resolve issues collaboratively.

Parenting styles also play a significant role in coparenting. Every parent has their own unique approach, and it is important to recognize that these differences are not necessarily right or wrong, they are just different, if they are within the range of acceptable. Respecting each other's parenting style without trying to force one style over the other provides a safe space for both parents to consult without fear or hesitation.

Focusing on common ground can build trust and create more stability for the children by collaborating and creating a consistent and supportive environment, one that accommodates both parenting styles while ensuring that the child's needs are met in both homes.

Involving children in these disagreements only adds unnecessary stress to their lives, so it is important to shield them from these adult conflicts.

Reflection Prompt: How do you and your coparent handle differences in parenting styles? Is there room for more collaboration, and how might that positively impact your child?

Anecdote

Imagine a situation where a parent hears their child complain about something happening at their other parent's home. The parent seizes the opportunity to ask their child what they would like to change. The child, feeling confused and torn, expresses a desire to live with the parent who offers a different approach. Without thinking through the long-term consequences, the parent then tries to use this complaint as a reason to change the parenting plan. As the situation escalates, the child becomes caught between two parents, both of whom want to "win." Regardless of the outcome, the child feels they have hurt one parent, causing emotional distress and confusion. They may even start to believe that sharing their true feelings will always lead to pain, making it harder for them to trust others as they grow.

In the end, the child is going to feel the burden of having created a battle of wills between the parents, just by expressing their feelings. The long term affects of this could lead to behaviours of repressing their feelings in the future, within different relationships.

Parenting through separation is one of the hardest journeys we take, and one of the most important. As tempting as it may be to lean on our children for insight, reassurance, or even direction, it is our responsibility to shield them from the weight of adult conflicts. Children do not need to know all the details, they just need to know they are loved, safe, and not responsible for fixing what the adults are working through. By keeping them out of the parenting time discussions, we protect their emotional development and strengthen our bond with them. We give them the freedom to simply be children, and that, in itself, is a profound act of love.

Final Reflection Questions:

Write an anecdote of your own describing how the children became involved in discussing the parenting plan.

1. **How did it affect the children?**

2. **How could you have handled it better?**

3. **What could your coparent have done differently to ease the pressure on your child?**

Your Personal Notes:

Chapter 6

The New Sandwich Generation – Children of Divorced Parents

"Children juggle invisible emotional loyalties, often without the tools or voice to express their burden."

For many years, we have talked about the "sandwich generation", adult children raising their families while caring for their own parents. But there is another group that deserves just as much attention and compassion. It is what I call the new sandwich generation: children of divorced parents - and their emotional experience is just as layered and complex.

These children are metaphorically "sandwiched" between homes, loyalties, expectations, and the ever-shifting terrain of blended families. While society often focuses on the logistics of divorce, parenting arrangements, financial support, or legal agreements, we tend to overlook the quiet, sometimes invisible, emotional burden carried by these children.

As divorce becomes more common, it is no longer unusual for children to grow up navigating two households, multiple parental figures, and a revolving door of stepsiblings. But what we must ask is: what does that feel like for a child?

For many, the answer is complicated, there are feelings of abandonment, confusion, and loss. There is often a deep desire to belong somewhere and the painful realization that they might not feel fully at home in either household. These children become emotional nomads, drifting between family units that may unintentionally make them feel peripheral or out of place.

Feeling Like a Guest in Your Own Family

One of the most heartbreaking realities for these children is that in both homes, they may feel like visitors. Even in the house of a biological parent, the introduction of a new partner, and potentially new siblings, can create a dynamic where the child becomes the outsider looking in.

Key: Children of divorced parents may feel like they do not fully belong in either of their homes, especially when new family units form around them.

When parents remarry and have children with their new partners, the child from the previous relationship may begin to feel that their place in the family is unstable. They might perceive their parents' attention shifting toward their new children or partner. The same happens when the other parent forms a new family, and soon, the child is standing on the edges of two tightly bonded units, unsure where they fit.

This emotional reality often plays out in subtle, painful ways. The child might notice that family traditions no longer include them, or that celebrations are scheduled without them in mind. They may even hear phrases like "our family" with the unspoken implication that they are not part of it.

In some cases, the blended family dynamic can be openly hurtful, with favouritism, exclusion, or even outright rejection. When one child receives a lavish birthday celebration, and another gets a card or hand-me-down, the message is clear: You are not one of us.

Reflection Prompt: Ask yourself, does your child feel as welcome, wanted, and included in your home as every other member of your household?

The Quiet Impact of Being Left Out

Children in this "new sandwich generation" may never voice their pain, not because it isn't real, but because they don't want to make waves. They may feel that complaining will only result in tension between their parents or will put them at risk of further alienation.

This silence can lead to a long-term emotional cost. Many of these children carry a profound sense of not belonging into adulthood. It can influence their self-worth, their trust in others, and even their future relationships.

Key: Children who feel emotionally excluded in their families often grow into adults who struggle with trust, connection, and self-worth.

In search of unconditional love, some of these young adults may rush into relationships, marriages, or parenthood. They may see starting their own family as a way to create the sense of belonging that was missing in their own childhood.

Sometimes, this urgency leads to poor decisions like choosing partners too quickly, becoming parents before they are ready, or staying in unhealthy relationships just to avoid being alone. The emotional scars of being the "extra" child in someone else's family often take years to surface, and even longer to heal.

Anecdote

A Personal Story

Let's revisit a real-world example that highlights this issue clearly:

My ex-husband had two more children with his new partner. She also had a son from a previous marriage. One day, my daughter asked for $2 at a garage sale to buy a toy, but her father refused, citing child support payments. When she asked to borrow it, his new partner said, "No, and you know why." Meanwhile, the new partner's child picked a toy freely that his mother paid for.

At Christmas, she watched her siblings open expensive gifts while she received thrifted, ill-fitting, and outdated clothing with thrift store price tags still attached. Worse, she was asked to wrap their new and pricey presents. One year, as a young girl, she was given a Santa-themed cutting board and knife set which she quietly re-gifted to them the following year.

She later talked about how deeply this hurt her and how invisible she felt in her father's home.

This experience was not just about the cost of the gifts, it was about the message that she didn't matter as much. These seemingly small moments had a seismic emotional impact.

Reflection Prompt: Even the smallest interactions like a denied request, a forgotten birthday, an awkward dinner table dynamic can leave lasting emotional impressions on a child.

How Can We Help?

Supporting children of divorce begins with awareness and recognizing that even when everyone is "doing their best," a child may still feel unseen, unheard, or unwanted.

Therapy and counselling can be incredibly beneficial for children navigating these complicated dynamics. But even when a child resists professional intervention, parents can still model emotional awareness by seeking their own guidance and learning how to parent from a place of empathy and stability.

Key: How parents integrate children into their blended families will have the greatest impact on how connected and valued those children feel.

Here are some ways parents can ease the emotional burden for their child:

- Prioritize consistent routines and open communication.
- Speak positively (or at least neutrally) about the other parent and household.

- Encourage a strong relationship with both parents, even when blended families are involved.
- Include the child in family traditions and make space for their preferences, not just the new partner's or step-siblings'.

The Role of New Partners

Blended families succeed or struggle largely based on how new partners approach the role. It is not uncommon to feel jealousy or discomfort about a partner's ex, especially when parenting time and attention are shared, but when those feelings are acted on with exclusion, judgment, or subtle undermining, the child suffers most.

Key: A new partner must understand that the child's other parent will always be in the picture, and that their role is to support the child, not replace a parent.

New partners should also be cautious about forming opinions based solely on the stories they hear. It is easy to take on our partner's resentment or bitterness, but doing so can lead to projecting those feelings onto the child.

Working the children into the new household can be as simple as taking an interest in their hobbies, making sure that there are things in the home that assist their hobbies, whether it be art supplies, related books, music, things they can bake with little assistance or lots of loving help.

Allow them to talk to you about their other parent and showing positive interest that does not make the child feel they are sharing too much or hurting anyone's feelings.

Reflection Prompt: If you are a new partner or stepparent, ask yourself: Am I allowing my own discomfort with the other parent to affect how I treat their child?

Creating a Home Where They Feel They Belong

Children do not need grand gestures, they need to feel seen, valued, and heard. That means inviting them to choose the movie on Friday night, including them in family photos. Asking about their favourite meals, and remembering that their voice matters.

It also means respecting the child's relationship with their other parent. This might be hard, especially when the coparent is difficult or unkind, but your child will always carry both of you in their heart. Never ask them to choose or pretend that parent does not exist when they are with you.

What If Your Child Tells You They Are Being Mistreated?

If your child shares concerns about how they are being treated in the other home, especially by a new partner, you must act.

Start by speaking directly with your coparent, not from a place of accusation but from concern. Be specific. Use your child's words, not your interpretations. Avoid turning the issue into a power struggle.

If that conversation does not lead to change, consider involving a counsellor or mediator, and if the situation continues or worsens, especially if your child's emotional or physical safety is at risk, seek legal advice. Their well-being must come first.

Key: Emotional mistreatment can be just as damaging as physical harm. Trust your child and take their concerns seriously.

The Long Game: Planning to Preserve Your Sanity

Being part of this "sandwich generation" means your children are carrying the weight of multiple households, two families, it is an exhausting place to live without a plan.

This is why structure is not just helpful, it is crucial, and it prevents new partners from throwing monkey wrenches into already existing working dynamics.

There is a reason I continually discuss parenting plans throughout the chapters of this book, it is essential for so many aspects of your new journey and all of the complexities of coparenting, so here we go again.

A parenting plan that considers children's needs across different ages and stages is a powerful tool in this context. It doesn't just serve the children, it serves the parent who is trying to hold everything together.

By knowing that parenting time will shift as a child grows, you can plan ahead emotionally, logistically, and even financially; but just as important, you prevent others from coming along and creating chaos.

When your plan outlines predictable schedules, holiday rotations, and age-appropriate transitions, it gives you room to breathe. You can schedule your own medical appointments, rest days, or time to perhaps support an aging parent without scrambling for childcare. And perhaps most importantly, you can do it without fear that someone will interfere.

This kind of structure also prevents decision fatigue. When the plan already answers, *"Who has the kids over March Break?"* or *"What happens when our child starts high school?"*, it removes a hundred small stressors that would otherwise pile up.

Key: A clear, forward-looking parenting plan offers stability not only to children, but to the parent juggling life's complexities.

Reflection Prompt: Are you giving yourself the same structure and compassion you offer everyone else?

Final Thoughts

The children of divorced families deserve more than just survival, they deserve belonging, connection, and a true place to call home.

It is up to parents, new partners, professionals, and communities to recognize the challenges they face and to respond with empathy and intention.

Final Reflection Questions:

1. **Have I truly considered how my child feels in each home?**

2. **Have I invited open dialogue with them, without defensiveness?**

3. **Am I contributing to their sense of inclusion or exclusion?**

4. **Write an anecdote where your child felt they didn't belong in one or both homes. What happened?**

5. **How did you respond at the time, and what would you do differently now?**

6. **What messages are your child receiving, directly or indirectly, about their place in each family?**

7. **List three subtle ways your child might be receiving a message that they are less valued than other family members. What could you do to counteract those?**

Your Personal Notes:

Chapter 7

Explaining Parenting Time to Children

Explaining parenting time to children can be one of the more emotionally delicate tasks after separation. Children often sense change before they fully understand it, and transitions can be unsettling, but with honesty, clarity, and empathy, this conversation can also become a doorway to reassurance and connection. Your words can help your child feel safe, loved, and secure during this uncertain time.

Be gentle with yourself as you approach this conversation, there is no perfect script, only your best effort, grounded in love and patience.

Honesty and Reassurance Go Hand-in-Hand

Explaining parenting time to children can be challenging, but it is crucial to be honest and clear. Children need to feel like they are part of the conversation, not just bystanders to adult decisions, while reminding them they have a voice, but adults make the decisions. Frame the situation in a way that emphasizes security and consistency. Reassure them of their importance and let them ask questions openly.

Over time, most children will adjust to their new routine and will recognize the love and support they still receive from both parents.

That said, it is not always easy to find the "silver lining." Each family's situation is different. Perhaps your child no longer has to hear the loud fights that once echoed through the house, or maybe an emotionally distant parent will now be more present and engaged.

Whatever the unique positives may be, highlight those that will resonate most with your child. Even subtle improvements can bring a sense of relief and hope.

Reflection Prompt: What are a few genuine positives about your child's new routine, no matter how small? Which ones might your child naturally notice or appreciate?

Age-Appropriate Conversations

Children process information differently depending on their developmental stage. A toddler might need simple, comforting language, while a teenager might appreciate more context and a chance to express opinions. What matters most is making sure your explanation is tailored to what your child can handle emotionally and cognitively.

Start with the basics: Explain that they will be spending time with both parents, but in two homes. Talk about their space and belongings in each home and reassure them that both parents will take care of them.

Reinforce love and stability: Children may feel uncertain or even blame themselves. Emphasize that they are deeply loved by both parents and that your love for them hasn't changed, only the living arrangements have.

Highlight the good stuff: Help them see the positives. Two cozy bedrooms. More one-on-one time with each parent. Unique routines or traditions in each household.

Invite questions: Let your child express their concerns and curiosities. Children often need repeated reassurances and clarification, especially in the early days.

Reflection Prompt: Think about your child's personality and age, what words or images would make the idea of two homes feel safe or even special to them?

Once you have thought about how to match your child's developmental needs, the next step is crafting the actual conversation, starting from the big picture.

Where Do You Start?

Sometimes, children need a bigger picture to help them understand the changes.

Age-appropriate examples:

0-3: "You will see mom on Tuesday and dad on Friday. We both love you very much." Keep language short, consistent, and positive.

3-5: Use visual aids like calendars and pictures of two homes. Offer simple explanations, like, "mom and dad live in different houses and you get special time in both."

6-12: These children may ask more questions. Be honest and allow space for feelings and leave out the details of the reason for the separation as discussed in Chapter 3, be reassuring and confident.

13+: Allow for input while affirming structure. "We know this isn't how you imagined things. If something doesn't feel right, we want to hear your thoughts. We will make any decisions, but your voice will be heard."

Explain separation or divorce simply: If they are old enough, tell them that sometimes parents choose to live apart. Gently but clearly reassure them that it is not their fault, and this is a decision made by adults to create a more peaceful and supportive environment for everyone. It is important that they understand they did not cause this so that they can understand it is not their job to "fix" it.

Normalize the situation: Let your child know that many kids live in two homes and that families come in all shapes and sizes. This is not unusual or something to be ashamed of, it is just another way families show love and care, by creating two, more stable, homes.

Reassure them of their worth: Children often internalize adult problems. Regularly affirm how valued they are and that their relationships with both parents will continue and be encouraged.

Let them know it is not forever: Kids may imagine "two homes" as a permanent, disorienting shift. You can gently explain that as they grow up, routines will change again. They will have more freedom and eventually choose how they want to spend their time, but while they are still living at home, they will have two loving places they belong. Most importantly, both parents will continue to listen and make changes that help them feel more comfortable.

Keep communication flowing: Remind your child that it is okay to come to you with questions or feelings at any time. Both parents are open to hearing how they are doing.

Reflection Prompt: Are there words you have used in the past to help your child understand tough topics? What metaphors or stories might help now?

In some families, parenting time looks very different from a 50/50 split. Let's explore how to talk with your child when time is not shared equally.

When Parenting Time Is Not Equal

When one parent has significantly more parenting time than the other, it is natural for a child to feel confused or even hurt. They may feel that things are unfair or wonder if one parent doesn't love them as much.

Here's how you can help:

Keep it simple: Always speak in terms your child can understand. Complexity adds anxiety.

Be honest but not heavy: Explain that the decision was made by the adults, and again, emphasize that it is not their fault.

Focus on what remains strong: Even if time is not split equally, both parents still love them deeply. They will still have special moments with each parent.

Explain the reasons: If one parent has less time due to work schedules or distance, explain that these are adult challenges that do not reflect love or preference. If the schedule was determined by the court or another professional, you can gently explain that those decisions were made to best support their needs right now and that schedules can change if circumstances do.

Example Script:

"You know how you've been spending more time at one house than the other? That's because of some adult things we had to sort out like work and making sure you are taken care of every day. It is not your fault. We both love you so much, and we're doing our best to make sure everything works well for you. If things change later, the schedule might too. Do you have any questions?"

Key: **The parenting schedule was chosen to meet the children's needs, not as a punishment or a preference.**

Reflection Prompt: How does your child tend to respond to feelings of unfairness? What words or reassurances have helped them in the past?

Some situations involve supervision during parenting time, which can raise new questions or concerns for your child. Here is how you could handle it with care.

Explaining Supervised Parenting Time

Supervised parenting time can feel especially confusing or even scary for a child. They may not understand why a third person is involved or what that means for their relationship with the other parent.

Here is how you might approach it:

Use gentle, clear language: Avoid technical or legal terms. Instead, speak about safety, fun, and comfort.

Be truthful but sensitive: You do not have to share details that are too heavy. Just say that another adult will be there to make sure everyone is safe and having a good time.

At the same time, if the child is aware of concerns and have experienced unsafe situations with the parent, this would be an opportunity to discuss how supervision is there to make sure those things do not happen and to provide them a safe place to enjoy the good experiences they have with that parent.

Reassure, reassure, reassure: Remind your child that they are safe and loved, and that both parents want what is best for them.

Explain the purpose: You might say that sometimes people get help to make sure things go smoothly and that doesn't mean something is wrong, it just means everyone is working toward the same goal: happy time together.

Example Script:

"When you spend time with mom, there will be another adult there too. That person is just there to help make sure everything goes great and everyone feels safe. It is called supervised time, and it is really just to make sure you have a good experience. We know it is a little different, but we love you very much and are here if you ever want to talk about it."

Let them know that supervised parenting time might change in the future, and that they can always ask questions.

It is okay if your child has mixed feelings. Some children may feel unsure or embarrassed; others might be afraid of what supervision means. Let them know it is normal to have questions or emotions about this change. What matters most is that they feel safe enough to talk with you.

Using age-appropriate language and allowing space for their emotions and questions will greatly assist them in managing this new environment while easing any anxiety they may feel with the supervisor's presence. If the child is hesitant about spending time with that parent, this kind of clear, gentle explanation can help alleviate concerns.

Reflection Prompt: What questions might your child have about supervised time? Are there any fears you can gently anticipate and soothe?

Explaining Structure with Heart

One of the greatest gifts we can offer children during and after divorce is a sense of predictability. When everything else may feel like it is shifting under their feet, having a clear understanding of when they will see each parent and knowing that this schedule is being followed helps build emotional security.

This is where a well-designed parenting plan shines.

Take, for example, a plan that divides parenting time into specific stages: infancy, school age, adolescence. Not only does this kind of plan reflect developmental needs, it also becomes a communication tool for kids. It answers questions before they are even asked.

“When will I see Mom next?”

“Will I be with Dad on my birthday?”

“What happens on Christmas?”

By using simple visuals, colour-coded calendars, or even stickers, younger children can grasp what might otherwise feel confusing. Older children and teens may appreciate a printed schedule or shared digital calendar that allows them to track and anticipate transitions.

- Colour-coded calendar
- Visual weekly schedule
- Special stickers for "transition days"
- hared digital calendars for older kids

When parents follow the schedule consistently, children learn that they can trust what has been agreed upon. That trust becomes the bridge that helps them feel safe and more open to communicating how they feel about transitions, plans, and their relationships.

Key: Children feel more secure when they understand the parenting time schedule and see it being honoured.

Reflection Prompt: Have you explained your parenting time schedule to your child in a way they can understand? What tools could you use such as visuals, calendars, and conversations to make it more concrete and comforting?

Anecdote

A Personal Story

When I shared with my children the parenting plan that we had agreed upon, including how holidays would be shared, they felt a sense of stability that they had not had living with the unknown and one parent's requests for them to influence situations.

Even when parenting time is not "equal," it can be made to feel fair, predictable, and respectful. Children find comfort in knowing what to expect and in knowing that their parents are not asking them to take sides or influence outcomes.

Now It is Your Turn

This is a chance to reflect with self-compassion, not judgment:

Write an anecdote of your own describing how explaining your parenting time to the children failed/succeeded.

- What went wrong/right? What did you notice in your child's reactions?

How did it affect the children?

- Were they confused or understanding, withdrawn or open, upset or relieved?

How could you have handled it better?

- Looking back, what might you change about your language, tone, or timing?

How could your coparent have handled it better?

- Was there room for more collaboration, clarity, or mutual messaging?

Final Thoughts

Explaining parenting time to your children is not about getting the words exactly right, it is perfectly okay if things do not go smoothly every time. It is about showing up with calm, clarity, and care. When your children see that you are emotionally available and always ready to listen, they will feel a deep sense of safety, even when life is changing around them.

Keep the lines of communication open and let them know they can always revisit the conversation whenever they need. In doing so, you are teaching them that love is a constant and steady presence, even as the world shifts. They will learn that no matter what, your love for them remains unchanged.

Remember, you do not have to get it right all of the time. What matters most is that you keep showing up, calm, consistent, and caring. Children do not need perfect, they need connection, and if you are reading this, you are already doing the hard work of learning how to build that.

Final Reflection Questions:

1. **What does your child most need to hear from you right now?**

2. **How can you reassure them not just once but over time?**

3. **What support do you need to stay grounded and confident as you guide them?**

Your Personal Notes:

Chapter 8

Building Cooperation Through Flexibility

Flexibility might not be the first word that comes to mind when you think about parenting after divorce. In fact, when things have been tense or unpredictable, flexibility can feel more like a risk than a virtue. But in truth, flexibility is the quiet superpower of peaceful coparenting. It allows us to meet the unexpected with openness, to support our children's growth and joy, and to model the kind of cooperative spirit we hope they will one day offer others.

Coparenting rarely follows a script. Life throws us curveballs like an unexpected work event, family emergencies, or special opportunities for the kids that happen to land on the other parent's time. In these moments, flexibility becomes one of the most valuable tools in a healthy coparenting relationship.

Of course, flexibility can feel vulnerable, especially if past interactions have been difficult, but approaching each situation thoughtfully can make a real difference.

Flexibility doesn't have to mean chaos. It means approaching each situation with respect, clear communication, and the intention to work together for the benefit of your children. It means knowing that plans might change and being willing to adapt when needed without guilt trips or defensiveness.

In this chapter, we will explore how to foster a spirit of cooperation with your coparent through thoughtful, flexible interactions.

Plan Ahead When Possible

If you see a scheduling conflict coming, bring it up as early as possible. Advance notice gives your coparent time to adjust their own plans and shows that you respect their schedule. Whether it is a work trip, a family gathering, or an invitation to a special event, planning ahead sets a collaborative tone. It also reduces stress for everyone involved, including your children.

Reflection Prompt: Think of a time when last-minute communication caused tension. How could early notice have changed the outcome?

Frame the Request Positively

Instead of making demands or pointing fingers, focus on the benefit for the children. Keep the tone light and collaborative. For example:

"Hey, there's a local science fair on your weekend and I think Rosie would love it. Would you be open to swapping weekends so they can attend? Totally fine if not just thought I'd check. Or, if you would like to take them yourself, I can provide all of the information and help with the other kids."

This kind of message shows that you are prioritizing the child, while also offering options and inviting input. It makes your coparent feel part of the decision-making process, not railroaded by it.

Reflection Prompt: Next time you make a request, can you offer two options instead of one? How might this change the dynamic?

Be Open to Compromise

Flexibility goes both ways; healthy flexibility is mutual. If it is consistently one-sided, it is okay to set firmer boundaries. If you are asking for a favour, be prepared to offer one too. Listen to your coparent's concerns and work together to find a middle ground, whether it is adjusting pickup times, trading weekends, or offering an alternative solution. The goal is mutual respect and shared problem-solving.

Compromise isn't always neat or easy but if both parents feel heard, it can still be a win.

Reflection Prompt: Have you ever insisted on a change without offering a compromise? What could you do differently next time?

Compromise does not mean losing, it means choosing peace and progress over pride.

Too often we associate compromise with weakness, as if giving an inch means losing control, but in coparenting, compromise is a sign of maturity and perspective. It says, "I care more about my child's needs than about being right." That is not weakness, that is leadership.

Communicate with Clarity and Kindness

Clear, respectful communication builds trust. Avoid accusatory or defensive language. Be honest about your needs but also express them in a way that is thoughtful. If your coparent raises concerns, try to respond with understanding rather than frustration.

Consider using "I" statements to reduce defensiveness:

"I'd really appreciate your flexibility this weekend so our daughter can attend her best friend's birthday party. I know it is your time and I'm happy to trade days if that helps."

Show Gratitude

If your coparent agrees to a change, thank them. A quick message expressing appreciation reinforces goodwill and encourages future cooperation.

"Thanks again for switching weekends, it really helped. The kids had an amazing time!"

Even small gestures of gratitude can soften interactions and build a cooperative rhythm over time.

Remembering Whose Time It Really Is

While practical flexibility is important, there is an even deeper layer to consider, one that asks us to look beyond the schedule and remember what this time really represents to our children.

In Chapter 4 we briefly touched on the importance of respecting the parenting schedule while also being open to reasonable changes. Here, we want to expand on that idea not just in terms of logistics, but in terms of perspective.

Parents often refer to the schedule as "my time" or "your time," but we need to pause and consider: **Whose time is it, really?** It is the children's time. It is their childhood which is precious, fleeting, and irreplaceable.

When a special event, opportunity, or meaningful moment arises, flexibility should be guided by one central question:

"If they would have been there, had it, or done it before the separation… should they be there, have it, or do it after the separation?"

This simple, powerful lens helps recenter our choices around what truly matters: maximizing the richness, joy, and connection in our children's lives. Children deserve continuity, spontaneity, and the ability to say yes to the experiences that light them up, just like they would have if their parents were still together.

This becomes especially important when the opportunity in question is a once-in-a-lifetime family event like a grandparent's milestone birthday, a cousin's wedding, or a family reunion where relatives gather from near and far. These are the moments that form a child's identity and memory bank. When children are denied access to these events simply because they fall on the "wrong" weekend, they are not just missing a party, they are missing part of their family story.

Reflection Prompt: Do you want your child to grow up flipping through family photo albums and asking, "Why wasn't I there? Where am I in this picture? Why didn't I get to be part of that day?"

That sense of exclusion can echo into adulthood and shape how children perceive their place in the family, and even their sense of belonging.

Of course, boundaries are important, and cooperation can't be one-sided, but flexibility does not mean surrendering structure, it means remembering that our loyalty should be to the child's best interest, not the parenting calendar. When both parents can hold this shared value, scheduling changes become less about who "wins" and more about what the child gains.

It is also why communication must be clear, respectful, and timely. If you would be open to your child attending a birthday party, dance recital, or hockey game during your parenting time, consider the same when it falls during your coparent's time. Flexibility rooted in fairness creates consistency and stability for the child in an otherwise shifting landscape.

Key: Children only get one childhood. Do not let a rigid schedule or a power struggle rob them of joyful experiences or cherished family memories they would have had if the family remained intact.

Reflection Prompt: The next time you are faced with a request, or needing to make one, ask yourself:

Is this something our child would have experienced before the separation? Will they look back and wonder why they weren't there? Let those answers help guide your response.

Delivery Matters

The tone and style of your request can make all the difference. Imagine you are asking a friend for a favour. Be casual, warm, and respectful.

Cooperative Example:

"Hey, a work friend is having a pool party for her kids on Saturday, and I think ours would love it. I could pick them up and bring them back the same day or we could trade weekends. Totally up to you, just wanted to ask."

Confrontational Example:

"I'm taking the kids Saturday. You never do anything with them anyway, so don't bother saying no. And if you do, forget about asking me for anything ever again."

The first version invites cooperation; the second demands compliance and stirs resentment.

Key: Requests that show respect are far more likely to get a yes.

When your coparent feels considered and respected, they are more likely to be accommodating. And when that respect is mutual, the coparenting relationship becomes much more manageable and even pleasant.

A Personal Story

At the beginning of my coparenting journey, I truly believed flexibility and cooperation were possible. I agreed to several arrangements I was not entirely comfortable with like having his new partner pick up the children on his days. I told myself it was about what worked best for the kids, and I still believe that.

But that spirit of cooperation was not always mutual. One Christmas, I surprised my son with tickets to his favourite hockey team on a weekend he was scheduled to be with his father. I asked to switch weekends so our son could go. Not only did he refuse, but he also threatened legal action. I later found out they had no specific plans that weekend, the refusal seemed to be about control, not the child.

I did not ask ahead, did not show the necessary respect for the schedule, because I wanted to preserve the surprise, but in hindsight, I put the moment I imagined ahead of practical communication. When my son looked at the unused tickets, silent and disappointed, my heart broke. I realized then how easily disregarding the need for communication can lead to hurt. And while I wanted to blame my coparent, I had to accept that it was my actions that led to the hurt.

That moment taught me something vital: excitement, surprises, and plans are never more important than clear, respectful communication. I learned to prioritize transparency over assumptions, and I've never forgotten the weight of that lesson.

You might face moments like this too, where your best intentions do not guarantee cooperation. It does not mean you failed, it simply highlights why clear communication and realistic expectations matter.

Reflection Activity:

Write an anecdote of your own:

- Describe a time when cooperation did not happen.
- How did it affect your children?
- How could you have handled it better?
- How could your coparent have handled it better?
- Do the same for a time when cooperation did happen.

These experiences, both the ones that went well and the ones that didn't, help shape how we approach coparenting. What matters most is what we learn, and how we carry those lessons forward.

The Bottom Line

Coparenting with flexibility does not mean always saying yes. It does not mean being a pushover or allowing constant disruptions. It means showing respect, staying open, and working together to create a stable, supportive environment for your children.

It is about choosing responsiveness over reactivity. Grace over rigidity. And partnership over point-scoring.

When communication is clear and respectful, children feel secure. And when parents can model cooperation, children learn to do the same.

Flexibility is not about keeping score or being endlessly accommodating, it is about building trust, modeling respect, and putting your child's life experience at the center. Every time you respond with grace, you strengthen the bridge between you and your coparent, and between you and your child's future. Even when cooperation is hard, your efforts matter.

Final Reflection Questions:

1. **How do you currently handle schedule change requests?**

2. **What could you do to make those interactions more positive?**

3. **How does your tone affect your coparent's response?**

4. **Are there opportunities to show more appreciation?**

Your Personal Notes:

Chapter 9

Structuring Communication with Coparents

"If there is one area where coparenting challenges show up early and often, it is communication."

Few things challenge us more in the early days of separation than communication. The person we used to share everything with now feels distant, defensive, or even dismissive. And yet, for the sake of our children, we must find a new way to speak. A structured, focused, respectful way

Effective communication is essential for successful coparenting. When parents establish clear guidelines and structures for communication while honouring one another's preferences and schedules, they help build a strong foundation for cooperation and mutual respect.

This might include using a shared calendar or online platform to coordinate parenting schedules and children's activities. It could also mean setting up regular check-ins (weekly, biweekly, or monthly) to calmly and constructively discuss issues related to the children's well-being, this often results in fewer surprises and less conflict.

It is important to maintain a respectful and professional tone in all communications, even when conflicts arise. Keep in mind: respectful communication doesn’t mean always agreeing. It means staying focused on the shared goal of raising healthy, secure children.

Reflection Prompt: When you speak to your coparent, imagine your child overhearing the conversation. Would they feel safe, supported, and loved by both parents?

Coparents should also be open to feedback and willing to adjust their communication styles, when necessary, where appropriate. This flexibility paired with consistency creates a pathway for trust, understanding, and collaboration to flourish.

By structuring communication clearly and consistently, coparents can reduce misunderstandings, demonstrate respect for each other's time and role, and model healthy relational habits for their children.

In any cooperative relationship, some degree of competition or disagreement is inevitable, coparents often have different ideas and values about how to raise their children. When your coparent seeks your cooperation on an issue, it is essential to remember that you do not have to agree with everything they propose.

It is perfectly reasonable to challenge their thoughts and offer alternative ideas as long as this is done respectfully. Coparenting is not about winning, being right, or proving the other parent wrong, it is about showing up with your ideas and listening to theirs, then working together to find a solution that best serves your children.

Three approaches I recommend; “I’m surprised”, “I’m confused”, and “help me understand”. All are non confrontational and not accusatory.

Anecdote

Imagine a situation where one parent asks for a variation to the parenting plan: they would like the children to attend a family reunion. The other parent, however, had planned to take the children to a special event that same weekend. It is easy for tensions to rise.

In these moments, the key is transparency and open communication. Both parents should share their reasons: What is the event? Why is it important for the children? Are there specific benefits or responsibilities attached?

With all the relevant information laid out, a child-focused decision can be made collaboratively, rather than through argument or assumption.

In a collaborative conversation, the parents can take into consideration the importance of each event and determine which one the children will either enjoy more or benefit from more.

Example: The parent who has scheduled time with the children may have made plans to take them to the zoo.

Considerations: The family reunion is a one-time event with family coming together from all over. If the children are unable to attend, they will miss the opportunity to meet family they may never have the chance to meet again, they will not be in family photos, and they will not be making memories that they can share with cousins and other family for years to come.

The zoo is open every day and available for another time.

Which event makes more sense from the children's perspective?

Now consider how best to communicate the request to the other parent.

Reflection Prompt: Construct a request that extends the meaningfulness of the event, the benefit to the children, and is respectful of not only the other parent's authority over their scheduled parenting time, but the disappointment they may experience at the thought of postponing their plans.

Key: Transparency and compassion are important when challenging the other parent's ideas. It builds trust, encourages compromise, and helps both parties focus on the child's best interests.

Staying Child-Focused

It is tempting to veer into personal conversations, especially when emotions are still raw from the breakup, but blending coparenting communication with personal issues can create discomfort, confusion, and distrust.

It is not always easy to draw a line between personal history and present parenting.

Coparents should avoid discussing personal matters like dating, finances, or how they spend their non-parenting time. These topics may trigger emotional reactions, distract from the children's needs, or lead to hurt feelings and communication breakdowns.

Reflection Prompt: Boundaries are not walls, they are clarity. By keeping coparenting conversations focused, you protect the space your children depend on.

To stay on track, establish communication boundaries. These might include:

- Using a designated parenting app or email only: Provide a clear, brief subject line. Keep each stream focused on that one central issue. Start new streams for other issues, this prevents potential confusion should a parent agree with issue A, leaving the other parent thinking the agreement was for issue B.
- Setting scheduled times for non-emergency discussions: Perhaps you set out specific days or times of day when both parents are prepared to receive communications, conversely, times that are communication free zones. One very important consideration is to agree that neither parent will start a conversation that could become conflicted while the children are in the other parents' care. This prevents a lonely or spiteful parent from upsetting the children's time with the other parent.
- Agreeing to keep all communication strictly about the children and the coparenting plan: It should be agreed that if a parent slips and tries to discuss personal issues one gentle redirection should be enough to end it.

This approach helps ensure both parents remain aligned on what truly matters: the children's school, health, development, and daily experience.

Key: Keeping communication strictly focused on the children avoids misunderstandings, builds trust, and reinforces shared purpose.

Real-Life Communication Examples

To help illustrate what respectful, focused coparenting dialogue looks like, here are a few real-world examples:

Example 1: Redirecting a Personal Conversation

Coparent A:

"Hey, just wanted to say I miss how things used to be between us. I know this is about the kids now, but can't we just be friendly again? Maybe grab a coffee sometime?"

Coparent B:

Thanks for reaching out. I hear that you're feeling nostalgic, and I do want our communication to feel respectful and cooperative.

That said, I'm working hard to keep our conversations focused on the kids so we can be the best coparenting team possible. Let's stick to discussing their upcoming schedule and needs.

Speaking of which, have you had a chance to review the proposed switch for Saturday so that Jordyn can attend her soccer tournament?"

Example 2: Responding to a Boundary Push

Coparent A:

"Wow. Don't you care anymore? We used to be able to just talk. This feels cold."

Coparent B:

"I do care, and I care deeply about making sure we create a stable, respectful coparenting relationship. Right now, the best way I can do that is by keeping our communication focused on the children.

I'm not trying to shut you out, I'm just reprioritizing. Let's make sure we're giving our kids the consistency they need. Have you picked up the medication for Ava, or should I grab it today?"

Example 3: Ignoring Personal Comments in High-Conflict Situations

Coparent A:

"Must be nice to have all that free time while I do all the work. I saw your new car, glad to know you're thriving."

Coparent B:

"Just confirming that I'll drop the kids at your place at 5 PM on Friday as planned. Please let me know if there are any changes to the weekend schedule."

By responding you acknowledge that you received the message, and by ignoring it and focusing on a child related issue, you make a statement that says you are not going to engage in conflict, but are very happy to coparent.

If you find yourself in a conversation that veers into personal territory, try acknowledging the comment briefly, then gently steer things back. For instance:

"I appreciate you sharing that with me, but let's focus on our parenting plan for the upcoming week."

Or: "I understand that's important to you, but right now we need to talk about our child's school project and how we can support them."

Over time, consistency with this boundary will help shape a clear understanding between both parents: personal lives are no longer part of the parenting conversation.

If the other parent continues to push, you can respectfully but firmly say:

"I understand that you may want to have a friendly conversation, but right now I want to keep our communication focused on the children. It is important to me that we stick to the parenting plan and ensure our children's needs are being met."

In more high-conflict relationships, you may need to ignore personal content entirely or inform the other parent that you will not respond to messages that include anything unrelated to the children.

If a communication has 3 points, 2 child related and 1 personal, respond only to the 2 appropriate points, remaining silent on the 3rd.

Key: Your coparenting relationship is different from your past romantic relationship. Your personal lives are no longer central to the conversation.

Coparenting communication can be the hardest part of post-divorce parenting. Sometimes it is like talking into a void. Other times, it feels like carefully stepping through a minefield. Either way, it often feels like you're the only one trying to keep it civil.

Key: Communication does not need to be warm, but it needs to be clear, respectful, and consistent.

Reflection Prompt: Ask yourself, 'Is this communication necessary, child-focused, and brief?' If not, it should not be sent.

If you've ever hit "send" on a message and instantly regretted it, same. We are human. There were days I crafted the perfect message, full of logic and fairness, only to be met with silence or sarcasm. It took me a long time to realize I was not going to be understood, and that was okay. I just had to be consistent.

Low-conflict communication does not mean silence, it means strategy. By using available tools like email, parenting apps, or shared calendars, you can stick to facts, be brief, and have a record of how your communication has progressed over time. You are not giving in when you stop arguing, you are choosing peace over proving a point.

One of the best decisions you can make is this: Stop trying to be right in your messages and started trying to be clear. Clarity becomes your ally. Emotional restraint can become your quiet form of power.

Key: Every time you disengage from chaos, you build trust with your child even if they do not realize it yet.

You are not weak for not responding. You are strong for knowing that silence can be stronger than a perfectly worded defence.

Verifying Who You are Really Communicating With

When coparenting through electronic means, it is easy to assume that the messages you receive are genuinely from your coparent, but tragically, that is not always the case and the damage can cut far deeper than we realize.

Anecdote

Personal Story

Many years after our divorce, I came to believe that during crucial periods of our children's lives, I had not actually been communicating with their father at all. It appears his new partner may have been impersonating him, responding to my emails and texts without his knowledge, shaping and sabotaging our coparent relationship.

I came to this not through suspicion, but by accident, years after it could have mattered. What this meant was, he would have had no idea about moments that had been pivotal in our children's development, moments where his presence, his acknowledgment, would have meant something.

This betrayal was not just about me feeling deceived; it created invisible cracks in our children's relationship with their father. They carried wounds they did not even fully understand, believing, at times, that he did not care, when if true, he had been deliberately kept in the dark. It created visible cracks in our coparenting relationship by allowing me to believe he did not have an interest in our children. Most damaging, I was following what I thought was advice and guidance from my coparent that was meant to help me in a parenting crisis; however, if it was not him the guidance appears meant to make the situation worse, which it did. Not only did it impact my life, but my child's life as well.

Key: Trust, once broken, leaves an invisible scar. Always verify important communication. Your children's emotional security depends on it being real, honest, and protected from outside interference.

If you ever sense inconsistencies like messages that seem unusually harsh, uncharacteristically distant, or simply "off", take it seriously. A quick phone call, a request to meet in person, can help safeguard your coparenting relationship from manipulation. It is not just about avoiding conflict with your ex; it is about preserving your child's right to have a true, uninfluenced relationship with both parents.

Conclusion

Healthy communication is not about perfection; it is about intention. By choosing clarity over control and focus over frustration, you are giving your child something powerful: a model of emotional maturity. That, more than anything, will shape how they learn to relate, resolve, and respect in their own lives and relationships.

Final Reflection Questions

1. **How do you currently communicate with your coparent? Is it working well, or does it often lead to tension or misunderstandings?**

2. **Are there moments when personal emotions spill into your coparenting conversations? What triggers those shifts, and how might you manage them differently?**

3. **Have you and your coparent clearly defined what topics are "coparenting only"? If not, how could you initiate that conversation?**

4. **Think of a recent disagreement with your coparent. Were the children's needs at the center of that exchange? If not, what shifted the focus?**

5. **How would your child describe your communication with the other parent? What would they say they feel when you are both speaking or not speaking?**

6. **How do you handle it when your coparent crosses a communication boundary? What is one respectful phrase or response you could use next time?**

Your Personal Notes:

Chapter 10

Rebuilding Trust: When Coparenting Feels like a Tightrope

“Trust is rarely rebuilt in a straight line. There may be setbacks, mistakes, and frustrations. What matters most is the overall pattern. One blip does not destroy trust but repeated disregard does.”

Of all the things that fracture during divorce, trust is often the hardest to rebuild and the most essential to your child’s emotional safety.

If you flinched reading the word "trust," you are not alone. After the hurts that often come with separation or divorce, trusting your coparent, or yourself, can feel impossible. This chapter is not about pretending everything is okay. It is about finding ways to rebuild trust where you can, protect yourself where you must, and always center your child's need for stability.

Trust Starts with Consistency

- **Show up on time**
- **Follow the parenting plan**
- **Communicate clearly and respectfully**
- **Follow through on promises**

One of the clearest ways to rebuild, or build, trust is through consistency. This includes showing up on time, following the parenting plan, sticking to agreed-upon routines, and communicating clearly. When you say you will do something and follow through, your coparent begins to see you as reliable, and if they do the same, you may begin to feel the early signs of rebuilding trust.

Trust is the invisible thread that holds coparenting together. It may not be seen, but it is felt in the small exchanges, the consistent follow-through, and the ability to let go of worry when your child is with the other parent. Without trust, coparenting becomes a tense negotiation instead of a collaborative effort. With trust, it becomes a shared responsibility that helps children feel safe, grounded, and supported in both homes.

For many, trust is one of the first casualties of divorce. Betrayal, hurt, resentment, these wounds run deep and often linger long after the separation. Rebuilding trust is not easy, and for some, it may never fully return, but in the context of coparenting, trust does not have to mean emotional closeness or friendship. It means having confidence that the other parent will act in your child's best interest, even when you no longer agree on much else.

Key: Trust is built over time through consistent actions, not words alone.

Reflection Prompt: You do not need to trust your coparent in all areas of life, only in the ways that relate to your shared responsibilities as parents. That distinction can be freeing.

When the Pattern Breaks: Rebuilding After a Trust Violation

Setbacks are common in coparenting. The key is not perfection, it is how you respond when trust is breached.

There may be times when your trust is broken, even after separation. Maybe your coparent fails to pick up your child on time without notice, or they make a unilateral decision without consulting you. These moments are difficult, and they require more than just frustration, they require boundaries and clarity.

Rather than retaliate or shut down communication, try to address the situation with firmness and clarity. For example: "When plans change, I need to be notified in advance, so our child feels secure." Focus on how the behaviour affects your child rather than how it makes you feel personally.

Key: When trust is broken, focus your response on your child's experience, not your personal hurt.

Reflection Prompt: Rebuilding trust after conflict does not mean forgetting the past. It means learning from it and setting clear expectations going forward.

Choosing Peace Over Proof

There is a particular frustration that comes when you know someone is lying, and you feel powerless to stop them. When your ex bends the truth and your child is caught in the middle, the urge to expose the lie can feel overwhelming. Perhaps they claim the children were sick and could not attend your scheduled time, or they insist they did not receive an important message you know was sent. In these moments, the instinct to expose the lie can feel overpowering. The desire to defend yourself, correct the record, or call them out may seem not just tempting but *necessary*. But here's the truth: urgently trying to prove someone is lying often only fuels the conflict and keeps both of you stuck in adversarial roles.

Coparenting is not a courtroom and it is not about winning or proving a case, it is about safeguarding your child's emotional well-being. Even if you are right, and even if the lie is damaging, escalating the conflict rarely benefits your child. There are calmer, more strategic ways to address dishonesty such as documenting the issue privately, setting clear boundaries, or seeking help through a parenting coordinator or mediator. Letting go of the urgency to prove a lie does not mean you are letting the other parent get away with something, it means you are choosing to respond rather than react.

Key: Letting go of the need to expose every untruth is not about ignoring reality, it is about choosing peace over power struggles.

Reflection Prompt: Sometimes the strongest move is not to strike back, but to step back so you can respond with clarity instead of emotion.

It is also important to remember that not all untruths are intentional lies. Human memory and perception are subjective; five people can experience the same event and walk away with five different interpretations. What feels like a lie to one person might genuinely be how another person remembers it. Misunderstandings, emotional filters, or incomplete communication can all shape how we recall and recount events. This does not excuse dishonesty, but it does open the door for questions. Before assuming malicious intent, it can be helpful to pause and consider that your coparent might simply see the situation differently or may have information that you do not yet have.

Let's look at a real life example that captures the emotional complexity and quiet strength required when trust is broken but handled with strength.

Anecdote

A Real-Life Moment of Strength

A few months after the divorce, Emily was looking forward to watching her daughter Chloe perform in the school winter concert. It was a simple event, but to Emily, it was a big deal. Chloe had practiced for weeks. According to the parenting schedule, Chloe was supposed to be with her mother that evening, but Emily's ex-husband, Mark, claimed there was a mix-up. He said Chloe was already with him that night and that Emily must have made a mistake.

Emily was confused and hurt. She checked her messages and calendar, she had not made a mistake, Mark had picked Chloe up early, knowing it was not his time. When Emily texted him asking about it, he doubled down and claimed Chloe didn't want to go to the concert anyway. Emily felt like she was being "gaslit".

Her first instinct was to call him out, forward screenshots of their agreement, and demand he apologize. She wanted to text mutual friends and tell them what he had done. But instead, she paused. She took a breath, sat with the discomfort, and reminded herself: *This doesn't need to be a battle right now.* Instead of engaging in a fight, Emily calmly documented the incident in her parenting journal and made a note to raise it with their parenting coordinator.

She did not get the evening she hoped for, but she also did not drag Chloe into the middle of an adult argument. That choice preserved Chloe's peace, and Emily's dignity.

Chloe never knew about the confusion, and that was the true success of the night. The issue was addressed and rectified with the help of their Parenting Coordinator.

Key: When you choose to step away from a power struggle, you create space for your child to feel safe and centered.

Reflection Prompt: There will be moments when you must surrender the need to be right to be the steady parent your child needs.

Not all coparenting situations are high conflict. In lower conflict or slowly improving relationships, there may be moments where trust can cautiously be offered again, and for the benefit of the child.

Choosing to Trust Even When It is Hard: The Difference Between Cautious Trust and Blind Hope

If your coparenting dynamic is slowly improving, or was never highly adversarial, there may be room for cautious trust to grow again.

Sometimes, trust must be extended before it is earned. This does not mean blindly trusting a coparent who has repeatedly let you down, it means cautiously allowing space for positive change, especially when your child stands to benefit from it. Letting a coparent take the lead on something small like attending a parent-teacher meeting or hosting a birthday party can be a first step.

Of course, this choice is not always safe or appropriate. In high-conflict or abusive situations, boundaries must be tight, and trust must be earned inch by inch, but in other cases, softening your grip on control can be a way of moving forward for you and your child.

Key: Sometimes, extending small opportunities for trust is a gift to your child not your coparent.

Reflection Prompt: Letting go of control does not mean letting go of care. It means trusting that you are not the only parent that can ensure your child is okay.

Important Note: In high-conflict or abusive dynamics, trust should not be assumed or rushed. It must be earned in small, verifiable ways, and only when doing so does not compromise safety. Your well being, and your child's, must always come first.

What Children See and Feel About Trust

Children are remarkably perceptive. They notice when one parent speaks poorly of the other, when promises are broken, and when tension fills the room during a handoff. When they sense that their parents trust one another, at least enough to share information and respect boundaries, they feel more secure.

Trust also extends to how you talk about your coparent when they are not around. Avoid making assumptions or comments that might damage the way your child sees their other parent. Children should never have to choose which parent to believe or love more. Even when your trust in your coparent is fragile, your child's right to a peaceful, loving relationship with both parents remains firm.

Key: When children see mutual trust between their parents, they feel safer, more loved, and less burdened.

Reflection Prompt: You are not just modeling trust for your coparent, you are showing your child how to build trust in all relationships.

Trust in Yourself

As vital as trust between coparents is, it cannot come at the cost of your trust in yourself.

You are doing your best. You are learning. You are adapting. Trusting yourself means giving yourself grace when things do not go perfectly. It means not second-guessing every decision or beating yourself up when a conversation goes sideways. Parenting, especially after divorce, is full of imperfect moments, trust yourself to grow from them.

No matter how rocky the path has been, each step you take toward trust-whether in yourself, your coparent, or your child's future, is a powerful act of love.

Trusting yourself does not mean having all the answers, it means knowing that your love for your child is your compass, and that even in hard moments, you are leading with heart, integrity, and care.

Key: Rebuilding trust after divorce begins with trusting yourself to move forward with clarity and care.

Trust won't look the same for every family but the effort to rebuild it, even in small ways, sends a powerful message to your child: that peace is possible, that stability matters, and that love can still guide the path forward.

Reflection Prompt: The journey to trust is not about perfection. It is about learning how to show up with steadiness, even in the face of uncertainty.

Final Reflection Questions

1. **Have you and your coparent established any consistent patterns that help build trust? What are they? If not, what small changes could begin that process?**

2. **What boundaries or expectations could you communicate to help prevent future trust breakdowns?**

3. **When has trust between you and your coparent been tested? How was it handled? How was it resolved?**

4. **In what ways might your child be affected by the level of trust between their parents?**

5. **Are there areas where you may need to extend trust for the benefit of your child even if it feels difficult?**

6. **Do you trust yourself to parent well through this season of life? What gets in the way of that trust?**

7. **If trust has been deeply broken, what steps are necessary to protect yourself while still showing up for your child's needs?**

8. **Do you trust your child's ability to speak for their own perspective about relationships, even when it differs from yours?**

Your Personal Notes:

Chapter 11

When Home Isn't Safe: Helping Children Heal from Family Violence

Childhood should be a time of play, wonder, and safety, but for many children, home is not a sanctuary, it is a place of silent fear, unpredictable moods, and emotional tension.

Violence in a home does not always arrive with a slam or a scream. Sometimes, it is the silence after a cruel remark, the flinch at a raised voice, or the way a child instinctively disappears when tension fills the room. Children notice everything, even when we believe they are too young or too distracted. They carry these moments like invisible weights, and those early experiences shape how they learn to love, to trust, and to feel safe in the world.

Family violence casts long shadows. Its impact on children can be profound, shaping not just how they feel in the moment, but who they become in the years ahead. In this chapter, we will explore the different forms of family violence, how they may affect children, and what parents and caregivers can do to support children who have witnessed or experienced abuse.

To support children effectively, it is important to first recognize the many ways violence can show up in a home.

The Many Faces of Family Violence

Family violence is not always obvious. It can be loud, yes, but often it is quiet. Subtle. Hidden behind everyday routines. Here are the most common forms:

• **Physical abuse**: Any use of physical force meant to control or intimidate, pinching, shoving, slapping, punching, or throwing objects.

• **Sexual abuse**: Any unwanted or coercive sexual act, whether directed at a child or witnessed by one.

• **Emotional abuse**: Words, gestures, or silence used to shame, belittle, or manipulate. This can sound like, "You're so stupid," or look like being ignored for hours, or even days, with what looks like 'the cold shoulder' or 'silent treatment', and is meant to control or manipulate the recipient.

• **Psychological abuse**: Persistent behaviours that erode someone's confidence or sense of reality, gaslighting, threats, or playing mind games.

• **Economic abuse**: Controlling access to finances, food, transportation, or basic needs as a means of domination, like not allowing a partner to use a jointly-owned car, or even one that is their own.

Often, these forms overlap, many children experience more than one type, directly or as witnesses. Even when the abuse isn't directed at them, the emotional impact can be just as severe.

Reflection Prompt: Have you witnessed or experienced any of these forms of violence in your childhood or your child's life? How were they explained, or excused?

When the Hurt Is Quiet: The Power of Invisible Violence

Not all abuse leaves bruises. Some of the deepest scars are emotional and completely invisible.

Invisible violence is the slow, quiet undermining of a child's worth: the eyeroll when they express joy. The sigh when they ask a question. The backhanded "joke" at their expense. Over time, these moments teach children that they are irritating, dramatic, or simply "too much."

Over time these quieter, chronic patterns like mocking, minimizing, dismissing, can make a child feel small and invisible. Over time, they may begin to believe they are annoying, too much, or not enough. A child who is constantly teased for "being too sensitive" may grow up questioning every emotional reaction they have. Think about it as a "slow burn" or "death by a thousand cuts".

These aren't just hurt feelings, they are developmental injuries that shape how children view themselves in every future relationship.

Reflection Prompt: Has your child ever stopped themselves mid-sentence, just in case it might make someone upset? Where did they learn to do that? Is it healthy self-reflection, or fear?

The Cost of Growing up in Violence

The effects of family violence on children are deep and often long-lasting. Some children may become anxious, withdrawn, or overly obedient. Others may act out, struggling with anger or impulsivity. They may have difficulty sleeping, concentrating, or connecting with peers. Some may develop depression or post-traumatic stress disorder (PTSD).

School becomes harder. Friendships become complicated. Trust becomes fragile.

Key: Children often absorb abuse as self-blame, even when they are not the target.

But the harm does not end in childhood. Children raised around violence may struggle to form healthy relationships as adults. They may internalize what they saw, believing love looks like control, or that yelling is just how people communicate. Some may become victims again. Others may become aggressors.

Key: Exposure to family violence will help shape the child's development and who they become as an adult.

How to Help Your Child Heal

Even if your child has been affected by family violence, there is still so much hope. Healing is not only possible, it is within reach, but it starts with intention and care.

Children do not just observe violence, they absorb it, and they often believe it is their fault. Even when they are not the direct target, the chaos and fear seeps into their development, influencing how they manage emotions, relate to others, and even understand love.

1. Provide a Safe and Supportive Environment

Children need to know that they are safe. That they are loved. That their world is no longer unpredictable or frightening.

This might mean removing them from an abusive environment, getting legal protection, or simply ensuring that home becomes a haven, not a battleground. Keep routines calm and predictable. Create space for peace and play. Most importantly, validate their experience.

2. Seek Professional Help

A trained therapist or counsellor can be instrumental in your child's healing. Therapy gives children a safe, confidential space to explore their feelings and experiences without fear of judgment.

It is vital that their sessions remain private unless there is a true safety concern. Children need to feel free to speak openly and to know their voice is respected.

Have you reassured your child that therapy is *their* space, not a place where they will get in trouble for being honest?

3. Encourage Open Communication

Children need to know they can come to you, even with hard things. You do not need to have all the answers. Sometimes, the most healing thing you can say is, "I'm here. You can tell me anything."

Try asking:

- "What are you feeling right now?"
- "Is there anything that's been bothering you lately?"

- “How can I help you feel safer?”

Create space. Be patient. They may not be open right away, but when they do, listen, really listen.

4. Support Positive Coping Mechanisms

Children process stress in different ways. Help them explore healthy outlets by drawing, journaling, dancing, mindfulness, outdoor play. Movement and creativity can be healing.

A therapist can guide you toward age-appropriate coping tools that you can reinforce at home.

What It Might Look Like in Your Child:

- They apologize constantly, even when they haven’t done anything wrong.
- They act “older than their age,” taking on adult roles like calming a parent. This is where we hear parents say, “He is very mature for his age.”
- They seem spaced out, detached, or “in their own world.”
- They suddenly hate going to school or have unexplained stomach aches, headaches, body pains, illness becomes a form of refuge or excuse.
- They overreact to small stressors or show no reaction at all.

These are not “bad behaviours”, they are survival strategies.

Even small acts, like making eye contact when they talk, or sitting beside them when they are sad, can slowly rebuild trust.

Key: Watch for changes in your child's moods, behaviours and participation in things that historically brought them joy or accomplishment. These can be indicators of distress that needs to be assessed.

Anecdote

Violence is not always loud

One afternoon, I casually said, "in a New York minute" while joking with my ex-husband. He stopped, scowled, and said coldly, "Why would you say something so stupid? What does that even mean?"

The air changed instantly. My children, who had been nearby, slipped away in silence. I remember the shift more than the details. But I'll never forget the look on my son's face as he backed away quietly, bracing for the next blow that never came.

That day stayed with me, not just because it stung, but because I saw how deeply it affected them. My kids weren't just learning to tiptoe, they were learning to survive.

Reflection Prompt: Have you noticed your children withdrawing when someone raises their voice? Do they rush to "make peace" even when it is not their fault? What do those behaviours tell you about what they have been exposed to?

Final Thoughts

Our children are not broken, they are adapting, they are growing in the shadow of something that never should have touched them, but it is not too late to help them grow in the light.

You do not have to be a perfect parent, they don't exist. You just need to be present. Gentle. Safe. You do not have to undo everything overnight, you only need to take the next right step.

Even if you could not protect them before, you can protect them now. Every moment of safety, every word of love, every effort to rebuild, is healing.

Let that be your legacy. Let your love be the thing they carry with them next.

Final Reflection Questions

1. **Write an example of your own describing how your children reacted to an instance of abuse.**

2. **How did that experience affect them in the short term and over time?**

3. **What could you and your coparent have done differently, even if you were doing your best at the time?**

Your Personal Notes:

Chapter 12

Easing the Transition: Helping Your Child Feel Safe and Connected

"Answering your children's questions thoughtfully is just the beginning. How you continue to interact with your coparent will also shape their adjustment."

Divorce brings about a wave of change, not just for the adults, but for the children who rely on stability and connection to feel secure in their world. As routines shift and living arrangements change, children often experience a mix of confusion, worry, and loss. These moments of transition, especially when one parent moves out, can feel unsettling or even frightening for a child. That is why the way you guide them through these changes matters deeply. Your calm presence, consistent communication, and continued cooperation with your coparent can provide the sense of safety your child so urgently needs.

Reflection Prompt: Think about your own experiences: How did your child react to the changes in your family dynamics? What signals did they give about their emotional needs during this time?

Children may experience feelings of loss and confusion, even if they still see both parents regularly. They might worry about their parent who is now living alone, feeling anxious about their safety, health, or loneliness. These concerns can manifest in different ways, some children may withdraw or become moody, while others may act out or express anger. Some might try to suppress their feelings, pretending everything is fine, while others may seek more attention from the parent they are currently with, becoming clingy or anxious.

Key: Every reaction your child has, whether quiet or loud, is a communication about how they feel.

Reflection Prompt: How did you notice your child's emotions showing up during this transition? Were they withdrawn, angry, clingy, or showing other signs?

As a parent, it is crucial to be aware of how your child is processing these changes and to acknowledge their feelings. Providing a safe space for them to express their emotions is key. Let them know that it is normal to feel sad or worried about the other parent but also reassure them that their parent is okay. Encourage regular communication with the other parent and offer suggestions for activities that might help your child feel more connected during these transitions.

Reflection Prompt: Have you been proactive in creating opportunities for your child to express their feelings, or have you noticed them holding things in? What changes could you make to offer more support during this time?

Supporting and facilitating regular contact with the other parent during your own parenting time tells your child, "It is okay to love both of us."

That alone can lift enormous emotional weight from your child's shoulders.

Reflection Prompt: Consider how you can maintain or encourage regular communication with the other parent to reassure your child. What practical steps can you take to ensure that your child feels connected to both parents?

The post-divorce period can be a challenging time for children as they adjust to the changes in their family dynamic. With patience, empathy, and support, children can learn to cope with their emotions and grow into their new family structure. Both parents have a considerable influence on how their child experiences these changes.

Key: Parents' emotions are not the child's burden. While we can't stop our children from feeling what they feel, we can help them adjust and cope.

Reassurance Without Emotional Burden

When a parent moves out after a divorce, it is important for the parent who remains in the family home to reassure the child that the other parent is doing well. This can be done by maintaining open communication between parents and encouraging the child to stay in touch as well. For example, if your child expresses concern for the other parent's well-being, offer to help them call or text to check in.

Reflection Prompt: How can you best reassure your child that the other parent is doing well? Have you been able to maintain open communication, and do you encourage your child to stay in touch with both parents?

If you learn that the other parent is doing well, be sure to share that information with your child. You might say something like, "I spoke with (your other parent), and they are doing great. They went out with a friend last night and had a good time." This lets the child know that their concerns are being addressed and that the other parent is managing.

It is important to stick to the parenting plan as closely as possible, as maintaining a sense of stability can reassure your child. If the other parent is not able to follow the parenting plan due to unforeseen circumstances, address the child's concerns by providing clear, age-appropriate explanations. If the other parent is struggling, let your child know that they are getting the support they need. For example, you might say, "Your mom is going through a tough time, but she is seeing a someone who is helping her feel better." Before sharing this personal step with the children, check in with the other parent and coordinate an acceptable message for the children that you are both comfortable with.

Reflection Prompt: How do you navigate explaining deviations from the parenting plan to your child? Are you finding ways to address their concerns while still supporting both parents' emotional needs?

Recognizing that honesty is important, it is equally important to show empathy and validate your child's feelings. Let them know it is okay to feel sad or worried about their other parent but also reassure them that both parents are adults with the tools to take care of themselves.

Reflection Prompt: What emotions do you think your child is processing as they adjust to their new family dynamic? How can you acknowledge those feelings while also providing reassurance that both parents are okay?

The parent who moves out can also reassure the child by staying in regular contact and maintaining their parenting time. When your child knows that you are still there for them, it can help them feel more secure.

If you are going through a tough time, it is okay to be honest with your child, letting them know that you are feeling sad or lonely but that you are taking steps to feel better, such as talking to a therapist or spending time with family and friends. It is important that you tell them it helps you feel better knowing they are with their other parent and enjoying that time with them. This alleviates guilt around transition.

This honest sharing of struggle should not be deep; but it can be helpful in normalizing emotions and letting them know that it is okay to share and it is okay to rely on others for help with all types of feelings.

Key: Honesty is not the same as full disclosure. Children need reassurance more than details.

Reflection Prompt: Are you being honest with your child about your emotions, without placing the burden on them to make you feel better? How do you find a balance between being open and not overwhelming them with adult concerns?

Be sure to follow through on any plans to see your child or speak with them. This consistency helps create a sense of security and reduces anxiety. Stability and trust through this upending period of their young lives can be measured in hours, minutes, when waiting for a parent to follow through on a plan, whether that plan is a designated phone call or a pickup time.

It is important to recognize that younger children are not apt to want to spend time on a telephone call, and consistency can be maintained by setting up a device allowing the parent to watch the child at play and participate by helping choose colours and seeing what the child is showing them. This can be a very effective method for engagement.

Key: Children should never feel responsible for the emotional well-being of their parents. Your emotional well-being is your responsibility, not theirs.

Managing Your Own Emotions

While it is natural to feel sad or lonely when separated from your child, be mindful of how you express these emotions. Saying things like "I'll be so lonely without you" or "I'll be sad until I see you again" might seem like harmless expressions of love, but they can have unintended consequences. These comments can make children feel as though they are responsible for their parent's emotions, creating unnecessary guilt or anxiety. Instead, try focusing on the positive aspects of their visit, letting them know how much you will miss them while also expressing excitement for what they will be doing during their time away.

Reflection Prompt: How can you express your emotions in a way that allows your child to feel loved without taking on the responsibility for your happiness?

When parents inappropriately express sadness or loneliness in front of their children, the child may start to feel like they need to "fix" their parent's emotions, which can add pressure and make transitions more difficult. It is essential to make sure your child feels comfortable in both homes without the burden of having to manage your emotions and without carrying the burden of guilt.

Key: Be mindful of what is said in front of the child about spending time away from them. Children should not feel responsible for their parents' emotions.

Reflection Prompt: What messages are your children receiving from your behaviour during transitions? How can you ensure that they feel loved but not responsible for your emotional state?

Overall Approach

It is important to be open and honest with your child about the changes in your family, but also to provide reassurance and support. By maintaining regular communication, sharing positive updates, encouraging adherence to the parenting plan, and showing empathy, you can help your child feel more secure and at ease during this transition.

Reflection Prompt: How can you create a supportive environment where your child feels heard, validated, and safe? What actions can you take today to support their emotional well-being?

Anecdote

A Professional Experience

As a Parenting Coordinator, I sometimes assist with transitions between coparents. While working with a parent who struggled to understand how their words were affecting their child during transitions, despite guidance to avoid saying things like “I’ll miss you so much” or “I’ll be sad until I see you again,” the parent continued to express their emotions in these ways, believing they were just showing love.

It was not until the child started having extreme emotional outbursts during a transition, refusing to go with the other parent because they felt guilty about leaving a sad and lonely parent behind, that the coparent finally realized the impact of their words. The parent acknowledged the mistake and was willing to change, but the emotional impact on the child was significant. This moment of self-awareness marked a turning point, and the coparent was able to adjust their approach, which helped repair the relationship and minimize further harm.

The parent started using recommended phrases like, “have a great time with dad, and I can’t wait to swap stories about all the fun we each had.” And “I am going to be so busy while you are with dad, maybe we can just relax together on Sunday and watch a movie.”

For younger children, if transitions become difficult at hand over, I recommend the other parent get the child from their seat, pick up from the floor/ground, but not from the parents’ arms. Often, it can be hand to hand that is creating anxiety in the child that may be unintended transfer of natural internal feelings of loss when the child is leaving their care.

If these techniques are not working, it may be necessary to try a third party they are also comfortable with, a grandparent, a family friend, someone that is familiar to the child.

Too often a parent will jump to the assumption that the child does not want to see the other parent, is afraid, not safe. However, children can become conflicted when seeing their other parent means leaving the one they are currently with, and not being able to resolve those feelings, or articulate them. Trying to resolve the concern before making hurtful or accusatory remarks will provide a more cooperative approach to trying to figure out what the issue is and how to move forward.

Transitions do get easier over time, especially when parents model resilience and emotional appropriateness. Children take their cues from us and the healthier the example, the faster they adapt.

Reflection Prompt: Consider a time when you noticed your words or actions affecting your child in a way you had not anticipated. What steps did you take afterward to help repair the situation?

Write an anecdote where your child expressed concern about both parents, and how you addressed it.

- How did your child respond?
- Were they comforted?

Divorce is not just a change in legal status, it reshapes your child's entire sense of stability. Using practical tools and insight to help your child feel safe and emotionally connected will help them adjust to their new reality.

Final Reflection Questions

1. **How have you expressed your emotions in front of your child during transitions? Did you register your child's reaction, even subtle?**

2. **How do you think your child has perceived these expressions?**

3. **What positive changes could you make to better support your child's emotional well-being during this time?**

Your Personal Notes:

Chapter 13

Letting Go of Labels: Focusing on What Matters in Coparenting

"It is about showing respect for your coparent and for yourself while creating a stable environment for your children."

It is natural to want to make sense of difficult coparenting dynamics. When communication breaks down or the other parent behaves in ways that feel manipulative, harsh, or chaotic, it can feel grounding to put a name to the behaviour. Diagnoses and labels may offer a temporary sense of control, but they often keep us stuck in conflict rather than helping us move forward.

We all know coparenting is a challenging and emotional experience, especially if you and your coparent have a strained relationship. It is common for coparents to want to understand their partner's behaviours, motives, and intentions to make sense of the situation and develop effective coping strategies. However, it is important to recognize that diagnosing a coparent's behaviours and motives may not be a productive use of your time and energy. In fact, it may even be harmful to your coparenting relationship and your own mental health.

The Narcissism Trap: Behaviours vs. Labels

Whether or not your coparent is a narcissist doesn't matter nearly as much as how they behave. Focus on patterns, not diagnoses. Describe what happens. Let the professionals assign labels, if needed.

Narcissism and abusive behaviour can be intertwined, but it is important to understand the differences between a narcissist and abuser with narcissistic traits.

Narcissists have a grandiose sense of self importance, a need for admiration, and a lack of empathy for others. They often have an inflated sense of their own abilities and accomplishments and may exploit others to get what they want. Narcissists, generally, have low self esteem. Narcissism is a personality disorder that is often rooted in childhood experiences, such as neglect or criticism, and is characterized by a pervasive pattern of behaviour across many areas of life.

An abuser with narcissistic traits, on the other hand, may exhibit some of the same behaviours as a narcissist but may not necessarily meet the criteria for a clinical diagnosis of narcissistic personality disorder. They may have an exaggerated sense of self importance, lack empathy for others, and be prone to grandiose or self-centered thinking, but these traits may be more situational and/or limited to their behaviour within certain relationships.

The distinction between a narcissist and someone with narcissistic traits is important because it affects how you approach the relationship and the potential for change.

Narcissists will be more resistant to change and less likely to seek help, as they often believe that the problem lies with others. A person with narcissistic traits may be more responsive to therapy and behaviour change interventions, especially if they are motivated by the desire to maintain their relationship or protect their family, selfish reasons that can benefit not just themselves, but others.

It is important to keep in mind that both narcissists and people with narcissistic traits can be emotionally manipulative and controlling, and it is essential to prioritize your safety and well-being if you are in a relationship with either type of person. Seek support from a therapist or counsellor who can help you navigate the relationship and develop strategies to protect yourself and your children if necessary.

It is crucial that in the absence of a confirmed diagnosis of Narcissistic Personality Disorder you avoid attempts to label the other parent with any of the professionals you deal with, whether mental health or the courts. It could backfire and put you in a defensive position appearing to be trying to manipulate the process. Stick to discussing the behaviours and allow the professionals, who are well experienced, come to their own conclusions and opinions.

Regardless of the label, the most important thing is to protect yourself and your children.

First and foremost, it is important to recognize that diagnosing your coparent's behaviour is not your job. Unless you are a medical doctor with specialized training and expertise, you are not qualified to diagnose your coparent's behaviours or motives and attempting to do so can lead to misunderstandings, miscommunications, and even false assumptions about them. That is going to make it harder for you to work together effectively and create a cooperative, positive coparenting relationship.

Moreover, trying to diagnose your coparent's behaviour can also lead to negative consequences for your own mental health. Constantly analyzing and interpreting your coparent can be stressful and exhausting and can even lead to anxiety, depression, and other mental health issues leading you to become distracted from your own well-being and the well-being of your children.

Instead of trying to diagnose your coparent's behaviour, focus on managing how it affects you. This means developing strategies and tactics for dealing with it, rather than trying to understand it. For example, if your coparent is consistently late for drop-offs or pickups, you might develop a plan for managing this time, such as setting consequences for lateness. This could be as simple as letting them know that going forward, when they are late, they will be receiving the children that many minutes later for the next transition. By letting the other parent know beforehand, they are making an informed decision when showing up late. If your coparent is consistently negative or critical, you might develop strategies for managing your own response to their behaviour, such as practicing mindfulness or seeking support from a therapist or support group.

Ultimately, managing how you respond to your coparent's behaviour is a more productive and effective way to coparent than trying to label it. By focusing on managing how you react or deal with it, you can reduce stress and anxiety, improve communication and cooperation, and create a more positive coparenting relationship. Remember that coparenting is a long-term process, and that it is important to prioritize your own well-being and the well-being of your children to create a successful outcome even it means "managing" the process on your end.

How Can You Do This

Many parents try to understand their former partner's behaviour by naming patterns that feel familiar or recognizable as buzzwords, such as narcissism or borderline traits which can sway which direction your coparenting flows, for example, imagine a parent named Danny who feels constantly undermined by their ex-partner during exchanges. Rather than focusing on specific behaviours, Danny starts referring to the ex as 'a narcissist' and begins anticipating hostility in every interaction. This focus on a label increases anxiety and resentment while providing no roadmap for managing the actual situations.

When you need to address your coparent's behaviour, aim to communicate clearly and assertively. Using "I" statements can help you express your feelings without sounding blaming or accusatory, for example, instead of saying, "You're always late for drop-offs," you might say, "I feel stressed and overwhelmed when I'm left waiting past scheduled drop-off times." Small shifts like these can keep the conversation calmer and more productive.

Try to stick to the facts when discussing coparenting issues. Avoid making assumptions about your coparent's intentions or speculating about their mental health. Keeping the focus on specifics helps keep the conversation clear and grounded.

When your coparent is speaking, make sure you are actively listening and trying to understand their perspective. Without interrupting or getting defensive, ask clarifying questions to make sure you understand what they are saying. If it isn't clear, or they were inappropriate, ask them to repeat it, or say it back to them and ask if that is what they meant to say. Give them the opportunity to reflect on what they said.

If the conversation starts to drift off-topic or becomes heated, gently guide it back to the current issue. It helps to avoid revisiting past conflicts or making personal attacks, even if emotions are running high.

What Can You Do When They Keep Going Off Topic?

If your coparent brings up a new topic, start by acknowledging their point and showing that you understand where they are coming from. You might say something like, "I hear what you're saying, but let's focus on the issue at hand right now."

Try to reframe the conversation in a way that connects it back to the topic you want to discuss. For example, if your coparent starts talking about their work stress, you can say, "I understand that work has been difficult for you, but let's talk about how we can make sure our child's needs are being met." This also works if they start talking about anything personal related to them, you, or your past relationship.

If your coparent continues to go off topic, be firm and restate your desire to remain focused. For example, you could say, "I appreciate what you're saying, but right now we need to talk about (issue at hand)."

If the conversation is getting heated or unproductive, it is okay to take a break and come back to it later. You might say something like, "I can't do this right now, I need a breather. We can talk about this again later after we both calm down?" If they refuse, it is okay to tell them that you are making the decision for yourself to end the conversation and offer an alternative time to come back to it.

If you are having difficulty communicating with your coparent, consider using a mediator to help facilitate the conversation. A mediator can help you both stay focused on the issues and communicate more productively.

Overall, it is important to try to steer the conversation back in a respectful and productive way.

- Acknowledge your coparents point.
- Reframe the conversation.
- Take a break when necessary.
- If all else is a struggle, consider mediation.

Key: Be adamant about keeping on track with the topic at hand without being offensive or defensive.

Anecdote

A Professional Story

During a conversation about their child's desire to play baseball in the upcoming season, dad tried to stay focused on the topic at hand, but Mom kept bringing up their past breakup. Despite dad's attempts to redirect the conversation, mom persisted, and the conversation became heated with dad reminding mom of the reasons for their breakup and telling her to keep her "Borderline" in check.

Unfortunately, the issue was unresolved, mom remained resentful of the label thrown at her, and the coparenting relationship was damaged. They eventually sought mediation, where I was able to help them stay on track and move past the issue; however, it took time for the coparenting relationship to rebuild from the damage that had been done during their previous interactions.

Write an anecdote where your behaviours may have caused a breakdown in communication.

How was it resolved?

What could you have done better?

Letting Go, Gently

Letting go of the need to label or explain your coparent's behaviour is not easy. It may even feel like you are letting them off the hook, but letting go does not mean you condone their behaviour, it means you are choosing peace over power struggles. It means you are stepping away from emotional quicksand and standing on solid ground.

If you have spent nights lying awake, replaying their words, analyzing their tone, and wondering what kind of person treats someone this way, you are not alone. So many parents come into this process carrying emotional bruises and scars. Wanting answers is natural, but what if the answer you are looking for is not about them?

What if it is this:

You do not need to understand them to protect yourself.

You do not need to fix them to parent well.

You do not need to diagnose them to heal.

That freedom of reclaiming your energy, your boundaries, your peace is available to you. Not because they change, but because you do.

Reflection Prompt:

Let's bring it closer to home. Ask yourself:

- When have I felt the urge to label my coparent instead of managing their behaviour?
- How did that impact my mood, my parenting, or my sense of self?
- What would shift in me if I stopped trying to figure them out and focused instead on what I need to feel calm and in control?

What would that look like, really?

Would it be fewer mental battles replayed in your head at night? More energy to spend with your kids instead of bracing for the next interaction? A deeper breath when their name pops up on your phone?

You deserve that, and your children deserve a parent who is not worn thin by someone else's chaos. One step at a time, let's choose energy over analysis, peace over power struggles, and presence over proving a point.

Final Reflection Questions

1. **What have I gained or lost by trying to understand or diagnose my coparent's behaviour in the past? Reflect on how this approach has affected your emotional well-being, your ability to parent, and the overall tone of your coparenting relationship.**

2. **When I focus on managing my coparent's behaviour rather than explaining it, what changes in my emotional response? Think about moments wherein shifting from analysis to action brought more peace or control.**

3. **What boundaries can I set to protect my energy and keep myself focused on what matters most, my children and my well-being? Consider emotional, mental, or conversational boundaries that could support your sense of calm.**

4. **Have I ever escalated a conversation by reacting to my coparent's provocation instead of staying grounded in the topic at hand? What might I do differently next time to stay aligned with my values and goals?**

5. **What do I need to remind myself of in heated moments to keep communication respectful and on track? This could be a mantra, an image, or a feeling that helps anchor you.**

6. **What would it look like to fully let go of trying to change or understand my coparent and simply focus on being the parent I want to be? How might that shift your daily experience, your stress levels, and your sense of freedom?**

7. **How can I measure growth in myself, not in their behaviour, but in how I show up for my kids, manage conflict, and protect my peace?**

Your Personal Notes:

Chapter 14

Parenting Through Power Struggles: Navigating Control, Conflict, and Abuse

"Every moment you choose inclusion over indifference, love over loyalty battles, you help your child grow roots that will nourish them for life."

Coparenting with someone who has been abusive, whether emotionally, physically, or psychologically—is not just difficult, it can be dangerous. It is draining and deeply personal. Yet, courts often expect you to treat it like any other parenting arrangement. This chapter is here to call that out and give you tools to manage, protect, and persist with empowerment. You do not have to befriend your coparent. You do not have to justify your fear. You only must stay focused on your children and on your own well-being.

Coparenting with someone who has been abusive is one of the most challenging and emotionally complex situations a parent can face. It calls for a balance between protecting your children, maintaining boundaries, and managing your own emotional well-being. If you find yourself in this position, it is important to acknowledge the strength it takes to show up for your children every day, while navigating an unpredictable and sometimes hostile dynamic.

The goal in these situations is simple, but not easy: keep the focus on the children's well-being, while minimizing their exposure to harm. This may require strong boundaries, clear documentation, and a deep well of patience. You are not in this alone support is out there, and you deserve it.

Supervised Parenting Time

In cases where there is a history of abuse, supervised parenting time may be necessary to ensure the children are safe. Supervision can come in many forms:

- A neutral, paid third-party agency location
- A trusted family member
- The other parent, if safe and legally appropriate
- A close family friend
- A paid supervisor who is present during time spent with the family
- Talk to your lawyer or court liaison about supervised parenting if there is any documented abuse.

As discussed in greater detail in chapter 14, whatever form it takes, the key is ensuring that the supervision arrangement protects the children while still allowing them to maintain a safe and positive connection with the other parent when possible.

Communicating with a Covert Opponent

Effective communication in this context is rarely about "fixing" anything, it is about staying calm, clear, and focused. Limit communication to topics that involve the children. Avoid responding to personal attacks or manipulative comments. These are bait, and responding to them only fuels the behaviour.

Try to use short, factual statements. Avoid defending yourself. Keep your tone neutral. A useful guideline is to assume that everything you write or say will be read aloud in a courtroom. Not only is this a good legal habit, it also helps you stay composed and focused.

- **Use BIFF: Brief, Informative, Friendly, Firm**

If communication becomes aggressive, end the exchange immediately. Your safety and your children's emotional security come first.

Using Grey Rock and JADE

Grey Rock and **JADE (Justify, Argue, Defend, Explain)** are communication techniques that help reduce conflict and protect your emotional energy.

- **Grey Rock**: Respond with minimal emotion. Be boring, neutral, and disengaged.
- **JADE**: Do not justify, argue, defend, or explain. Just state your position and stop.

These techniques help prevent power struggles and reduce the emotional payoff for the abuser.

But be aware: abusers sometimes learn these techniques, too, and try to turn them around on you.

Reflection Prompt:

- You never have to accept disrespect simply because you share children.
- Boundaries are not barriers to your children's love, they are shields from harm.
- You are allowed to protect your peace, even if others do not understand why.
- Healing is possible for you and for your children.

Structure as a Shield

- When you're coparenting with someone who is emotionally abusive, controlling, or manipulative, structure is not just helpful, it is essential.
- A well-crafted parenting plan that includes detailed, age-specific schedules and clear boundaries is not about rigidity, it is about safety. It reduces the opportunity for arguments, ambiguity, and manipulation. For example, when a plan outlines exact times, locations, and methods for exchanges, there is less room for last-minute power plays or controlling behaviours.
- In high-conflict situations, a parenting plan like this also helps ensure children are not drawn into adult conflicts. Instead of relying on frequent communication between parents, the plan itself carries the decision-making weight. This reduces the need

for ongoing negotiation, and in turn, lowers the child's exposure to stress.

- Even holidays, birthdays, and school events are addressed in advance. Rather than negotiating year after year, the plan sets expectations from the start. It offers something else that can be hard to come by in these dynamics: emotional breathing room.
- When the plan is followed, it is not just a legal document, it is a promise. It says, "This is how we protect the kids. This is how we keep the peace."

Key: In high-conflict or abusive dynamics, a clear and detailed parenting plan minimizes contact, reduces conflict, and protects everyone involved.

Reflection Prompt: Does your parenting plan reduce the need for constant interaction with your former partner? Are there areas that still leave room for conflict or manipulation and how could you strengthen those boundaries?

Protecting Your Children

Above all else, your job is to protect your children from harm. That responsibility does not go away just because a court order expects coparenting. Here are practical steps to help protect your children:

1. **Document everything:** Record incidents of abusive or inappropriate behaviour. Dates, times, and brief factual descriptions are key.

2. **Set firm boundaries:** Boundaries protect both you and your children. These might include restricting direct contact, requiring third-party communication apps, or setting up supervised parenting time.

3. **Keep the door open for your children:** Let them know they can talk to you if they ever feel uncomfortable. Make it clear they are not responsible for either parent's actions.

4. **Create a stable, supportive environment:** Your home can be a healing space. Consistency, warmth, and structure help children feel safe.

5. **Seek help for yourself:** Therapy is not just for the kids. A therapist can support you in navigating the emotional landmines that come with coparenting with an abuser.

Managing Your Own Emotions

Your ability to stay grounded affects everything, your children's stability, your interactions with the other parent, and your overall health. Emotional regulation is not about repressing your feelings; it is about creating space to process them in healthy ways.

1. **Make time for self-care:** This can be as small as a morning coffee alone, a walk with a friend, or a journal before bed.

2. **Let go of what you can't control:** You won't change your ex's behaviour, no matter how reasonable you are.

3. **Find your people:** Whether it is a support group, a friend who understands, or a therapist, connection matters.

4. **Stay child-centered:** When the situation gets tough, ground yourself in your love for your children. That love is your compass.

Key: Remember to prioritize your own self-care to ensure that you can provide the best possible support for your children. With patience, persistence, and a focus on what's most important, you can help your children.

Coparenting with an abuser can be challenging, but it is essential to prioritize your safety and the safety of your children. When communication is necessary, it is important to remain calm and focused on the children's needs. Stick to the facts and avoid getting drawn into arguments or personal attacks. Always use "I" statements to express how you feel and avoid blaming or accusing statements. It is important to set boundaries around communication, if your coparent becomes aggressive or threatening in the conversation, end the communication, then seek support from a therapist or counsellor. Protect yourself by keeping a record of all communication, including text, emails, and voicemails. If any boundaries are crossed, such as threatening behaviour or harassment, seek legal assistance to protect yourself and your children. Remember, your safety and the safety of your children should always be your top priority when coparenting with someone who is abusive.

Example: Abusive Message

"I got the kids from school today and they are all coughing and sneezing, you obviously aren't taking care of them. Why would you send them to school like this? You have no idea how to be a parent so I'm taking them to the doctor now."

As most parenting plans will have a requirement to respond within a certain time frame,

Suggested Response:

"Thank you for letting me know the children are not feeling well. Please let me know what the doctor says."

This response defuses the conflict and models mature, child-focused communication. It also prevents the other parent from pulling you into a defensive conversation.

Another example:

Instead of saying:

"You made me feel uncomfortable at soccer practice."

Try:

"I was not comfortable with the way you approached me at the soccer field. I do not want to be approached at the children's events."

This avoids blame and keeps the focus on your boundary. If the behaviour continues, follow up in writing and keep a record.

There might still be an inappropriate response, such as, "That's your problem" or "Get over it", "Grow up and get your head straight for the children".

There is no need to respond to any of this, you simply walk away. If the other parent continues the behaviour after you have requested that they stop, and it was through a face-to-face conversation, send the request electronically so that it is documented. After this, persistent behaviour that you have requested a stop to can be dealt with legally if necessary.

Key: Communication is not a conversation, it is documentation.

Remember, there is no authentic coparenting relationship when there is or was abuse.

Crafting a Parenting Plan with an Abusive Coparent

Creating a parenting plan with someone who has been or still is abusive can feel daunting, but it *is* possible to create one that protects your children. Here are a few tips:

- **Get help:** Work with a legal professional experienced in high-conflict parenting.
- **Be specific:** Clearly outline parenting schedules, exchange details/locations, communication methods, and boundaries. Vague language invites manipulation.
- **Stay calm:** Do not react emotionally when negotiations get difficult. Do not take "the bait" you both know how to push each others' buttons.
- **Plan for safety:** Use public locations for transitions or third-party supervisors.
- **Expect Pushback:** Set boundaries anyway.

- **Build in Accountability:** Use court approved communication apps.

Key: Be clear, be calm, and be willing to ask for legal help. Your children's safety and emotional health must guide the plan.

Litigating with an Abuser: Preparing for the Long Game

Family court can be overwhelming, especially when your coparent thrives on chaos or manipulation. Stay steady with these strategies:

- **Work with a skilled lawyer:** This is not a time to go it alone.
- **Document everything:** If it is not in writing, it didn't happen. Even contemporaneous notes are beneficial, keep logs and notebooks.
- **Flag safety concerns:** Do not minimize. If something feels unsafe, say so.
- **Stick to facts:** Avoid emotional stories. Present clear, concise evidence.
- **Lean on support:** Friends, therapists, and professionals can help you through the long process.
- **Be patient:** Litigation is often slow and emotionally draining. Prepare yourself and pace your energy.
- **Be Prepared:** your story is valid, but court wants evidence.
- **Be Clear and Detailed:** Focus on timelines, tone, and tangible facts.

Key: Present evidence, not emotion. Let your documents speak louder than your fear.

Parallel Parenting Overview

Parallel parenting is often a necessary strategy when coparenting with an abusive coparent, especially if direct communication is too emotionally charged or unsafe. This method involves setting up a parenting plan that minimizes contact between the parents, reducing the opportunity for conflict or manipulation. The focus is entirely on the children's needs, and both parents have clear responsibilities and expectations for their roles.

Key Features of Parallel Parenting

1. **Limited Communication:** Communication is reduced to what is absolutely necessary and is typically done in writing, such as through email or a parenting app. This helps avoid verbal confrontations and ensures a record of all exchanges.

2. **Clear Boundaries:** Each parent maintains their own distinct role, and there is less overlap in decision-making. The parenting plan could specify which parent is responsible for certain decisions (e.g., schooling, medical care, extracurricular activities).

3. **Independent Decision-Making:** Instead of attempting to negotiate or collaborate on every decision, parents follow their individual responsibilities and only involve the other parent when absolutely required. The less direct interaction, the better.

4. **Avoiding Personal Interactions:** Where possible, exchanges of the children should take place in neutral, public places to limit personal interaction such as daycare, school, or a third party. This helps to reduce the potential for emotional manipulation or abusive behaviour during exchanges.

5. **Structured Parenting Time:** Each parent sticks to the agreed-upon schedule without making changes at the last minute, time swapping only when necessary and/or beneficial to the children. The more structured and predictable the time spent with each parent, the safer it is for the children emotionally.

Benefits of Parallel Parenting with an Abuser

- **Safety for the Children:** It reduces the chance of exposure to conflict and manipulative behaviours.
- **Emotional Relief for the Parent:** By minimizing direct interactions, the parent can focus on providing a stable environment for their children without being emotionally drained or drawn into battles.
- **Clearer Boundaries:** The structure of parallel parenting enforces boundaries that protect everyone involved, including both parents and the children.

Final Reflection Questions

1. **What boundaries have I set that are working well and which ones need adjusting?**

2. **How can I better document and protect myself without feeling overwhelmed?**

3. **What communication strategies have helped reduce conflict so far?**

4. **Who can I count on right now for steady, nonjudgmental support?**

5. **What can I do this week to nurture *myself*, not just my children?**

Your Personal Notes:

Chapter 15

Dating after Separation: Introducing New Partners to Children

"Managing our own emotions with care allows our children to stay children and free to grow, love, and adjust without unnecessary emotional weight."

For parents, the heart often moves faster than the healing. Starting over can bring excitement and a sense of hope; but for children, a parent's new relationship can feel like a fresh loss. Too often introductions happen too fast or with little regard for the child's emotional readiness, and the consequences can last for years.

This chapter outlines a practical, trauma-informed protocol that has worked with hundreds of families under my guidance.

Divorce can be a difficult and emotionally challenging time, especially for children. Amidst the emotional upheaval, parents must find a way to navigate a new chapter in their lives without causing unnecessary harm to their children. Coparenting after divorce demands thoughtful, intentional decisions, particularly when it comes to introducing a new partner into a child's life.

This is a stage that is often filled with excitement and hope for the parent, but uncertainty and even fear for the child. The prospect of blending lives again may feel like progress to the adults; but to the children, it can feel like yet another disruption, a reminder of what has already been lost.

Introducing a new partner to children after divorce can be challenging for everyone involved. It is essential for parents to be mindful of their children's feelings and needs during this transition. The good news is that establishing clear guidelines and boundaries can create a smoother and more emotionally safe experience for everyone.

Key: Children view "moving on" though a very different lens than adults, often as a loss, not a gain.

A Child-Focused Protocol: Time-Tested and Trauma Informed

Many years ago, I developed a highly effective protocol that involves implementing an incremental process that has consistently delivered a secure and healthy transition for children adjusting to their parents' new lifestyle. This is not just a theory, it is a time-tested, child-focused approach that I have shared with hundreds of families. The process is designed with built-in safeguards to ensure the well-being of the children.

Key: The children's safety and emotional well-being should always be prioritized over the parent's desire to quickly move forward with their new relationship.

New Partner Protocol: The Six-Month Buffer Model

- Wait at least six months after you are physically separated before introducing new partners to your children.
- Be in a romantic relationship with your new partner for no less than six months before any introduction is considered.
- Avoid leaving children alone with the new partner until at least six months after the introduction.

This may seem conservative to some, but these timeframes are based on years of observing what works and what leads to emotional fallout for children. Divorce is a traumatic experience for many children, and introducing a new partner too soon can exacerbate feelings of loss, confusion, and instability.

It is essential for parents to provide their children with time to adjust to their new family structure before asking them to accept another person into their daily lives. This transition should be viewed from the child's perspective, what feels manageable to an adult can feel overwhelming to a child.

Introducing a new partner too soon after separation can be overwhelming for children and may cause them to feel that their parent is not fully committed to them or their family. Children often silently grieve the loss of the family they once knew and when a parent introduces someone new prematurely, it can feel like that grief is being ignored or erased.

Similarly, waiting until you have been in a romantic relationship for at least six months before introducing your children to a new partner gives you time to assess the relationship more clearly. It gives space for the initial excitement to settle. The mask of new love, the carefully curated best behaviour, often begins to loosen over time. This period allows you to witness how your partner responds to stress, how they manage conflict, and how they treat others, all of which can influence how they might eventually treat your children.

Once the new partner is introduced, parents must be mindful of how they involve their children in the relationship. While it is important to allow the relationship to develop naturally, parents must also take steps to ensure that their children are comfortable with the new partner. It is crucial that a parent remains present during the initial six months following the introduction. This allows the parent to closely observe the partner's interactions with the children, assess their tone and level of patience, and monitor the children's level of comfort and adaptation to the new individual in their lives.

Always having eyes and ears on for six months provides the parent with valuable insights. Children are perceptive and they may notice the subtle shift in a partner's tone before you do. They may spot a dismissive look or hear a sigh that speaks volumes. Just as someone new to your life can maintain a mask for only so long, the same applies to the way they relate to the children.

Key: The third part of the protocol should not be rushed and holds the utmost significance, possibly having the greatest impact on the relationships going forward.

Parents should be clear about their expectations and establish boundaries around how the new partner interacts with their children. Open and honest communication can help create a smoother transition and ensure that everyone involved feels comfortable and supported.

Being complacent about the way your new partner treats your children can have lifelong effects on your relationship with your children. It may not be evident in the beginning, but children remember. They remember who made them feel small, who dismissed their discomfort, and who did not protect them when they needed it.

Reflection Questions:

- Have you ever witnessed or experienced a moment where your child clearly showed discomfort with a new partner?
- How did you respond, and in hindsight, would you do anything differently?
- What can you do to ensure that your children feel safe, heard, and protected in these situations?

Before introducing a new partner to the children, I recommend that the parent has a conversation with the new partner. During this conversation, the parent should give the new partner permission not to feel obligated to love the children 'as if they were their own' and reassure them that they understand that this may not be possible. This approach prevents the new partner from feeling pressured to put on a facade of being overly attentive or affectionate towards the children, which may become unsustainable over time.

Should this happen, and the new partner gradually settles into a more natural and genuine interaction with the children, the children may misinterpret any reduction in attention or affection as a sign that the new partner no longer likes them. This may cause the children to blame themselves and wonder if they have done something wrong.

Key: Children have a keen sense of perception when it comes to subtle changes in adult behaviour and may often internalize the burden of blame for those changes.

Introducing children to too many potential new partners can also have negative consequences. Over time, as new partners come and go, children may become reluctant to emotionally invest or allow themselves to connect. This emotional distancing may provoke a negative response from a new partner, ultimately creating a self-fulfilling prophecy of a strained relationship.

After having this conversation with the new partner, together you can decide if this is the right time, the right approach, or whether this is even a responsibility the new partner is ready for.

Key: Introduction to the children can be just as stressful for the adults, and it is incumbent upon them to carry the burden of making sure it is done well.

Reflection Prompt:

- How might your new partner feel about taking on a role in your children's lives?

- Are you both ready for the emotional complexity this could bring?
- What boundaries or expectations should you clarify together beforehand?

It is important to remember that introducing a new partner to children is a significant step that requires communication and collaboration between parents. Parents should be clear about their expectations and establish boundaries. It is also important to listen to the children's feelings and concerns and address them with compassion.

When parents decide to introduce a new partner to their children after a divorce, they should communicate openly and honestly with each other. Communication is the foundation of successful coparenting and can make the process of introducing a new partner smoother for everyone involved.

It is crucial to inform the other parent of the impending introduction of a new partner to the children. This is not a request for permission, nor an opportunity for veto. The purpose is to ensure that when the children talk about the new partner, the parent doesn't respond with shock or dismay, responses that could signal to the children that they have done something wrong or disloyal.

Additionally, such a reaction may lead children to believe that they have hurt the other parent's feelings. Worse still, they may no longer feel safe sharing future concerns about the new partner should they have any.

Key: It is essential that children feel safe and at ease discussing what is happening in each parent's home with either parent, without fear of any negative consequences or retribution.

Parents must remain open to hearing how their children feel about life in the other parent's home. If a child shares a concern, listen without defensiveness. Determine whether it is a manipulation attempt or a valid issue needing attention. Keep the child's well-being at the center of every response.

New partners should never attempt to replace a child's parent. Doing so may cause loyalty conflicts and stress for the child, while also damaging the coparenting relationship. The goal is not to erase the past but to build something new with respect for what came before.

Instead, a new partner should focus on forming a positive, supportive relationship with the child, one built on mutual trust, time, and authenticity. Respect the role of the biological parent and find ways to connect with the child that feel natural and sincere.

New partners should never replace the role of the biological parent during significant "firsts" or special moments in a child's life. Events such as first bra shopping, prom shopping, or the first fishing trip or round of golf are milestones that belong to the parent-child relationship.

These moments are woven into the fabric of the child's emotional development and bonding. A new partner, while important, should respect the sacredness of these moments and allow the biological parent to be the one to participate.

The child should not feel that their connection to their biological parent is being overshadowed or diminished by the introduction of someone new. This respect for "firsts" ensures that children can navigate the emotional complexities of family change without feeling as if they are losing precious memories or moments with their parents.

Key: New partners do not automatically enter the coparenting relationship as an equal partner to the parenting plan. They enter the child's life as a guest and their role and influence must be earned through trust and respect.

Be Mindful of Labels

One subtle but powerful way parents can support their children through this transition is by being mindful of the language they use when referring to their new partner.

Children should not be expected to use labels like *stepmom*, *stepdad*, *bonus parent*, or *chosen family* prematurely, or at all. These titles imply a level of closeness, authority, or emotional connection that may not yet exist. Assigning labels too soon can make children feel pressured to accept someone before they are ready to or to pretend they are comfortable when they are not.

Instead, refer to your partner by their name and allow your children to define the relationship at their own pace. Let the language evolve naturally, if and when the connection deepens. This respectful approach gives children the time and space they need to adjust without emotional coercion.

Using neutral language also helps children avoid feelings of disloyalty to their other parent. Being forced to label someone new in a parent-like role can provoke internal conflict, especially if the child feels that embracing the new partner means betraying the parent who is not present.

If your child asks, 'Is she my new mommy/daddy?' you might respond; 'She is someone important to me, but you already have a mom/dad. You can decide how you would like to think of him/her when you get to know them.'

Key: Language shapes relationships. Give your children the dignity of choosing how they describe the people in their lives.

When the Other Parent Moves Too Fast

One of the most challenging moments for a parent after divorce can be discovering that your coparent has introduced a new partner to the children far earlier than you feel is appropriate. Whether the new partner is someone unfamiliar to the children or the relationship itself is still fresh, this sudden change can stir up strong emotions for both you and your kids.

But what matters most in this moment is how *you* respond.

Stay Calm in Front of the Children

No matter how frustrated, shocked, or hurt you may feel, try not to let those emotions spill out in front of your children. They are already managing the complexity of shifting family dynamics. Seeing you remain steady, even if the situation feels unjust, sends a powerful message: *We're going to be okay.*

If you need to vent, do it privately with a friend or therapist. Your children do not need to absorb adult stress, they need reassurance that their world remains stable and loving.

Avoid Badmouthing the Ex or Their Partner

It may feel tempting to make a sarcastic comment or offer a harsh judgment, but doing so can confuse or distress your child who may feel caught in a loyalty bind. They might worry that liking the new partner would hurt you or feel guilty for disliking the situation and be unsure who it is "safe" to talk to.

Instead, model respectful neutrality, even if it is hard. You can say, *"It sounds like you met someone new at your other parent's house. If you ever want to talk about it, I'm always here to listen."*

This keeps the door open for communication without forcing an opinion.

Create Safe Dialogue So Kids Can Share Discomfort

Sometimes children feel unsettled but do not know how to express it. They may be unsure if it is okay to admit they are uncomfortable or they may worry they will upset one of you.

Make it easier for them by offering open-ended, nonjudgmental questions:

- "How did it feel to meet someone new at your (other parent's) home?"

- "Is there anything you'd like to share about your time there?"
- "What would help make things feel more comfortable for you?"

Let your child know their feelings are valid and that they do not need to protect you by keeping them hidden.

Recognize Signs of Harm vs. Mere Discomfort

It is important to distinguish between normal discomfort, such as awkwardness around a new adult, and signs that something deeper is wrong.

Mere discomfort may look like:

- Shyness or quietness around the new partner
- Preferring to spend time alone when the new person is visiting
- Asking questions about who the person is or why they are there

Signs of harm or emotional distress may include:

- Sudden behavioural changes (e.g., aggression, withdrawal, nightmares)
- Comments that suggest fear, inappropriate behaviour, or emotional pressure
- A refusal to return to the other parent's home without explanation

If you are concerned about your child's safety or well-being, keep a record of what they say and seek advice from a trusted professional such as a therapist, pediatrician, or legal advisor.

Anecdote

Consider this real-life anecdote: a father introduced his children, a son 12 and a daughter 8, to his new partner while still in an intact marriage with their mother, even bringing her home for a "sleepover" while mom was in hospital. This was explained to the 8-year-old daughter as equivalent to her having a playdate or a friend sleep over.

On another occasion, while the mother was at a family function, the new partner brought her 13-month-old son for a trip to the zoo together. Being 8, the daughter was excited to go to the zoo, the son being 12, realized that this was inappropriate and refused to go, staying at a friend's house for the day. The daughter has since told the mother that she felt anxious and uncomfortable at the zoo and was vomiting, but at the time she did not understand why.

Introducing a new partner to children while still in a relationship with their other parent can cause confusion, anxiety, and feelings of betrayal.

It can also expose them to potentially inappropriate situations and have a significant impact on their emotional and psychological well-being. It is crucial for parents to be mindful of the potential consequences of their actions on their children, especially during a challenging time such as separation or divorce.

Parents should be aware that children will have a completely different experience in relation to their new partner depending on how and when they are introduced. Whether positive or negative is up to you as a parent.

What is the bottom line?

Exposing children to premature relationships can have serious and long-lasting consequences on their emotional and psychological well-being, regardless of your status with the other parent. Children can experience confusion, anxiety, feelings of betrayal, and other negative emotions when they are exposed to their parents' infidelity or new partners before separation or divorce has been finalized. Children need stability, consistency, and a sense of safety and security during this difficult transition and involving them in inappropriate situations can disrupt this sense of stability and security.

I have heard parents rationalize the introduction as knowing the children will be happy to see them happy, but this is not how the children experience it as they live in the pain and confusion left behind.

Furthermore, when parents involve their children in their personal relationships and decisions, it can create a sense of burden and responsibility for the children, who may feel that they need to take sides or choose between their parents. This can be an overwhelming and stressful situation for the children to navigate, and it can have long term affects on their relationships with their parents, and in their own future romantic relationships.

Overall, it is important for parents to prioritize their children's well-being and to avoid involving them in their personal affairs. They should strive to create a safe and stable environment for their children during the difficult transition of separation and divorce.

Reflection Prompt:

- What were the red flags that this introduction was not appropriate or well-timed?
- How did the children respond in the short and long term?
- What would you do differently if given the chance to go back?

Note: While the guidance provided here outlines a structured and effective process for introducing new partners, it is important to acknowledge that each family is unique. Some parents may follow these steps and still find their child struggling, while others may do very little preparation and seem to have few complications. Just because there is no visible resistance does not mean the child is unaffected. Children rarely speak up, but they always take it in.

Final Reflection Questions:

1. **Are you prioritizing your child's emotional needs over your desire to move on?**

2. **Have you created space for your child to express how they feel about your new partner?**

3. **How can you maintain a balance between moving forward in your own life and ensuring your child's emotional stability as they adjust to new family dynamics?**

4. **Have you had any discussions with your children about how they are experiencing you moving forward with a new life?**

Your Personal Notes:

Chapter 16

Parenting Plans That Grow with Your Child: A Developmentally Informed Approach to Time Sharing

Parenting time is not one-size-fits-all, it should grow and adapt just like your child does. In this chapter, we explore parenting time recommendations tailored to different developmental stages, followed by a sample parenting plan to help you create your own. These suggestions are built on years of family law experience and child development research, offering both structure and flexibility to meet your family's unique needs.

Newborn to Age 4: Building Attachment and Predictability

- Frequent, short visits to support bonding with both parents
- Transitions occur every 2–3 days, ideally during calm parts of the day
- Holiday time shared in shorter, manageable blocks
- Exchanges occur in a consistent location with minimal disruption

Ages 5 to 9: Fostering Stability and Routine

- Regular weekly schedule, typically alternating weeks or 5-2-2-5 pattern

- Midweek contact (calls or short visits) for continuity
- Detailed holiday rotation (Christmas, Thanksgiving, birthdays, etc.)
- Set pick-up and drop-off times with clear school-year transitions

Ages 10 to 14: Encouraging Responsibility and Independence

- Continued structured schedule with some room for flexibility
- Child's input begins to be considered in minor scheduling adjustments
- Shared responsibility for extracurriculars and school support
- Communication boundaries established, parents use agreed-upon methods (e.g., email or app)

Ages 15 to 18: Honouring Autonomy and Connection

- More flexible parenting time with teen involvement in planning
- Plan still respected as a baseline, but with accommodations for social, academic, or work demands
- Clear expectations around curfews, transport, and shared responsibilities
- Teen has access to both parents as desired within the framework

Why This Works:

This approach supports the child's developmental stage while also helping parents plan and reduce conflict. Structure evolves as the child grows, just as parenting should.

Parenting Plans are more than schedules, they are tools to create consistency, reduce conflict, and support your child's development at every stage. Whether your child is in diapers or applying to college, your parenting plan should reflect their needs and your shared goal: a secure, peaceful childhood.

Crafting a parenting plan requires careful thought and collaboration. I have provided a sample parenting plan to give you a broad perspective of what an effective one might include. Remember, this is not a one-size-fits-all solution but rather a guide to inspire and assist you in shaping a plan tailored to our family's unique needs. A comprehensive parenting plan addresses key areas such as communication, responsibility sharing, and the evolving needs of your child at different developmental stages.

Key: We ask our children to do something we would not, live in two homes at the same time, be mindful as you set their schedule.

Your Personal Notes:

Sample Parenting Plan

THIS IS A PARENTING PLAN DATED THIS 10th DAY OF February, 2023

Between

Annie Hasaway

(Annie)

AND

Hank Willoughbethere

(Hank)

1. Background

1.1 Hank and Annie began to cohabit in 2010

1.2 Hank and Annie were married on April 5th, 2012.

1.3 They separated on September 29, 2018. The parties will continue living separate and apart.

1.4 They have 2 children of the marriage, Holly Hasaway, born June 16, 2009 ("Holly"), and Alfred Hasaway, born July 23, 2012, ("Freddie"), also referred to as "the child" or "the children".

1.5 They agree to be bound by this Document which settles all current parenting issues between them.

2. Parenting

2.1 Hank and Annie will enjoy Shared Parenting Time as follows;

Option 1- Parenting Schedule for Children over 9. At this stage, children are better equipped to manage longer stretches away from either parent, making alternating week schedules more viable.

i) Hank and Annie will have a week-about schedule with transitions every Friday after school or at 8am if school is not in session.

I prefer a week-about schedule to begin on a Friday, it offers a relaxed transition from one parent/environment to the other providing a lot of time together to settle into the week's routines.

ii) Transitions will take place at the drop off/pick up at school.

iii) If transitions are outside of school drop off/pickup they will drop the children off at the other parents' home or an agreed upon location.

Option 2- for children from ages 4-8, the 5-2-2-5 schedule provides for limited transitions and even though there is a 5-day stretch, it is over a weekend which can be a very busy time seeing not only the parent but extended family mitigating much of the potential for anxiety.

The child(ren) would have parenting time with one parent every Monday/Tuesday, the other parent every Wednesday/Thursday, and alternating weekends

Transitions would be effective at morning drop off of the parents' scheduled day, meaning, when the Monday/Tuesday parent drops off at school Wednesday morning, the parenting time/responsibilities of the Wednesday/Thursday parent would begin. This would alternate the start of parenting time/responsibilities every other Friday.

This is a preferred parenting plan, allowing for consistency not only for the children making it easy for them to remember whose "day" it is, but also for the parents allowing them to have the freedom to commit to non-parenting activities/work on a consistent basis every week.

iv) Hank will have parenting time every Monday and Tuesday from Monday morning drop off through to Wednesday morning drop off.

v) Annie will have parenting time every Wednesday and Thursday from Wednesday morning drop off through to Friday morning drop off.

vi) Hank and Annie will alternate weekends from Friday morning drop off through to Monday morning drop off starting with Annie the first weekend after signing the Parenting Plan.

If the parents already have a weekend rotation, we will include that.

Option 3- for toddler children we like to look at more frequent transitions, such as 2-2-3, to allow for more frequent parenting time with each parent as discussed in Chapter 4.

vii) Week 1-Annie will have parenting time from Monday morning drop off through to Wednesday morning drop off, and Hank will have parenting time from Wednesday morning drop off through to Friday Morning drop off.

viii) Week 2-Hank will have parenting time from Monday morning drop off through to Wednesday morning drop off, and Annie will have parenting time from Wednesday morning drop off through to Friday Morning drop off.

ix) Hank and Annie will alternate weekends from Friday morning drop off through to Monday morning drop off starting with Annie the first weekend after signing the Parenting Plan.

For infants there must be a very detailed and situationally focused plan that allows for daily or near daily contact with both parents, as is feasible, desired, and safe.

I'm now going to run through holidays and special occasions. I am most familiar with Canadian holidays, I will focus on those, but this can be adapted to the similar holidays in any country.

2.2 Family Day/President's Day

Option 1- we use this line when neither parent is invested in the holiday, or when the parents are so high conflict that only the major holidays are shared or rotated keeping opportunities for conflict as limited as possible

(a) This holiday will be enjoyed by the parents scheduled to have parenting time.

Option 2

Parenting Time will follow the regular schedule. Should this holiday fall on a parent's scheduled weekend and they wish to keep the children through the holiday time to Tuesday morning they will notify the other parent no less than 30 days prior, and the other parent will not make plans with the children for that Monday until after the 30-day deadline.

Option 3

Hank and Annie will alternate this holiday from after school/work Friday through to Tuesday morning drop off with Hank in odd years and Annie in even years.

School Spring Break

Option 1

(b) This holiday will follow the regular schedule.

Option 2

Hank and Annie will alternate the option to have the children for the entire Spring Break, Hank will enjoy odd years and Annie even years.

The holiday period will include the 5 weekdays and the scheduled parents' weekend.

Option 2 Possible inclusion for families with a Week a Bout

If the timing of the Spring Break creates a situation for that parent to have 3 consecutive weeks, the other parent will enjoy one overnight during the week following the March Break, on a night agreed upon by both parents. If no agreement is reached no less than 10 days prior to the first day of March Break the parent exercising the overnight will have final choice. The parent who is enjoying the March Break will not make plans for the week after until the other parent notifies of their chosen night.

We include some flexibility where the parents can make room for the children to maximize their Spring Break by spending it with the parent who is not scheduled to have them if the scheduled parent is working, and the other parent is able to provide them and experience. Keeping in mind always that this is the children's time, their childhood, and their Spring Break.

Easter Weekend

Option 1

(c) Annie will enjoy parenting time with the children from after school/work on Thursday through to Tuesday drop off at school in even years.

Hank will enjoy parenting time with the children from after school/work on Thursday through to Tuesday drop off at school in odd years.

Option 2

Hank will enjoy parenting time with the children from after school/work on Thursday though to 4pm on Saturday, and Annie will enjoy parenting time with the children from 4pm Saturday through Monday morning in even years and will alternate in odd years.

Mother's Day

Option 1

(d) If the children are not otherwise with Annie this weekend, she will enjoy the full weekend with them from Friday after school through to Monday drop off at school.

Option 2

If the children are not otherwise with Annie this weekend, she will enjoy time with them from Saturday night drop off at (an agreed upon time after dinner) through to Monday morning drop off.

Mother's Day and Father's Day are often emotionally charged. Dropping children off the night before can reduce anxiety and create a more relaxed start to the special day.

Option 3

If the children are not otherwise with Annie this weekend, she will enjoy time with them from **(pick a time frame that works for the two of you)**

Option 4

If the children are not otherwise with Annie this weekend, she will enjoy time with them for no less than (set number of hours, let's assume you choose 4 hours) 4 floating hours. The hours to be communicated to Hank no less than 7 days prior and Hank will not make plans for any time that day until Annie notifies him of her requested time. Hank does not have the option to veto or deny Annies chosen 4-hour time frame.

The floating hours allow flexibility from year to year accommodating potential variations to how you plan to spend your special day.

Victoria Day Weekend

(e) **Options as laid out in Family Day, but ensure you detail them for each holiday.**

Father's Day

(f) **Reverse of Mother's Day, be consistent to avoid future conflict, if possible**

Canada Day

(g) **Options as laid out in Family Day, but ensure you detail them for each holiday.**

Civic Holiday

(h) **Options as laid out in Family Day, but ensure you detail them for each holiday.**

Summer

Option 1

(i) The children will share their time with the parents as follows:

(i) Hank and Annie will each have the option of 2 uninterrupted weeks with the children.

(ii) The 2 weeks may not be consecutive until the summer of 2025

Parents will often feel that 2 weeks is too long of a period for the children to be away from one parent, and when they are younger, I agree. To be proactive and so that parents are not faced with conflict in the future, include a trigger date for an agreed upon age that the youngest child must be to move to consecutive weeks, usually when the youngest is 9 or 10.

(iii) Neither parent will choose a week that overlaps the other parents' Annual Family BBQ, dates to be provided no later than 30 days prior to the other parents choosing their summer dates.

Addressing historic annual events ensures consistency for the children to participate. It is important to be clear and detailed to avoid conflict.

(iv) Annie will have the first choice of weeks in even years and Hank in odd years.

(v) Both parents will take into consideration any arrangements for the children's summer activities when planning holidays, i.e. sports, etc.

(vi) Both parents acknowledge that the summer vacation is for the enjoyment of the children and that any unreasonable inflexibility will have a negative impact on them.

(vii) The parent who has the first choice of vacation time with the children will notify the other no later than May 1, and the other parent will reciprocate no later than May 15.

Choose "no later than" dates that work with your jobs/situations.

(viii) All other weeks will follow the regular schedule.

Labour Day

(j) **Options as laid out on Family Day, but ensure you detail them for each holiday.**

Thanksgiving Weekend

Option 1

Many families have set days when they gather for their family dinner and have already accommodated both sides of the family, choose the days and times that make sense for you.

(k) Annie will enjoy Thanksgiving with the children every year from Saturday morning at 10am drop off through to Sunday morning at 10am drop off.

Hank will enjoy Thanksgiving with the children every year from Sunday morning at 10 am through to Tuesday morning drop off.

Option 2

Many parents have alternated within their family as a regular course, you would alternate the weekend so that the children can enjoy a family meal alternating sides every year.

Halloween

(l) This holiday will be enjoyed by the parent scheduled to have parenting time.

If the parents are cooperative and maintain a relatively healthy relationship I will include;

The parent not scheduled to have parenting time may attend to take pictures or join for the first part of trick or treating as agreed upon by the parent with scheduled parenting time.

Christmas/New Year

(m) Christmas will be shared every year as follows

Option 1

The children will be with Hank from December 24 at 2pm to December 25 at 2pm in even years, with Annie in odd years.

(ii) The children will be with Annie from December 25 at 2pm through to December 26 at 2pm in even years, with Hank in odd years.

(iii) Each of the parents will accommodate the others work schedule to ensure that they each have a 24-hour block of time.

(iv) The remaining holiday days will follow the regular schedule.

Option 2

(i) The children will be with Hank from December 24 at 2pm to December 26 at 2pm in even years, with Annie in odd years.

(ii) The remaining holiday days will follow the regular schedule.

Option 3

It is okay to get creative here if you are both accommodating and flexible. It is important to be very detailed, not as agreed upon, no vague, no deciding later. Christmas is one of the most emotional and contentious holidays for coparenting.

Options for the Jewish Holidays

Passover

Hank will enjoy no less than 2 nights with the children from after school/work beginning the night before the day of the holiday.

Rosh Hashanah

Hank will enjoy no less than 2 nights with the children from after school/work beginning the night before the day of the holiday.

Yom Kippur

Hank will enjoy this holiday with the children from 5pm drop off at dads through to drop off at Annie's home after the breaking of the fast.

Hannukah

This will take a lot of flexibility and cooperation, keeping in mind that if one parent is Jewish and the other is not, do not take more time than necessary from the parenting time. For those years there is an overlap with Christmas, it is important to prioritize both holidays for the parent who historically celebrated, and whose family still does.

Option for Muslim holiday

Eid

The parent not scheduled to have parenting time for Eid will have parenting time the following day, or, the second day of Eid, as follows.

(i) from after school through to the following day at 9am if on a school day or;

(ii) from 9am through to 6pm on a Saturday/Sunday/holiday.

Children 's Birthday

(n) The children will spend time with their parents scheduled for parenting time.

(o) The parents acknowledge the importance of communication on special days for the children's healthy development and relationship maintenance.

2.3 If one parent agrees to a flexible variation to the parenting plan allowing the other parent to take the children for a longer period of time, and then reneges on that agreement causing the other parent to incur a financial loss, the parent who reneges will reimburse the other parent in full within 7 days of receiving valid receipts that are nonrefundable and applicable.

2.4 Annie and Hank acknowledge that the other is a devoted and loving parent and that it is in the best interest of the children to have a close relationship with both parents.

2.5 The children's best interests will always be the most important factor in making decisions about them, understanding that each parent may not agree on best interest and have autonomy to parent their way on their parenting time.

2.6 Both parents recognize that any level of tension between them creates an emotionally stressful situation for the children, both agree that in the best interest of the children, they will ensure that:

i) they are encouraged to love and respect both parents and extended family.

ii) they receive whatever supportive counseling is recommended and that the parents participate in their own counseling to address the emotional issues related to the separation as they may arise.

iii) they will discuss any parenting issues directly with each other, without using the children as messengers and they will do so when the children are not present. When the children are present, they will speak to each other in a respectful manner. Communication may take place via telephone if agreed upon by both parties.

iv) they will make all reasonable efforts to ensure each feels comfortable when attending functions for the children.

Communication

Option for high conflict parents

2.7 Hank and Annie will communicate through a recognized communication app unless under the direction of a 3rd party professional to shift to an alternate, supervised option. Text may be used for emergencies or traumatic evenst followed up by a phone call if necessary.

2.8 Both parents will check the app no later than 6pm every evening.

2.9 Neither parent will send any non-emergency communications to the other after 10pm or before 6am.

2.10 If a parent receives a communication, they will acknowledge receipt of the communication and, if they are unable to provide an adequate response at that time, provide a reasonable time by which they can respond.

2.11 The children can contact the other parent upon request, no reasonable request will be denied, understanding that there are times that it is not appropriate, such as when the children are facing consequences or otherwise engaged with family time.

2.12 When an issue arises, the parent first made aware will share the full details of the issue with the other parent, including any documentation/communications, with a request for feedback on next steps. The receiving parent will provide feedback within 24 hours, preferably, and a plan will be discussed as to how best to move forward as coparents, and with any other third party that may be involved, i.e. school, coach, etc. If the other parent is unavailable, the parent may address any timely situations in the interim. Conferring between the parents may require a telephone call, if agreed upon, or with the presence of a 3rd party professional.

2.13 Neither parent will communicate to the children the plans made by the other parent that does not affect their parenting time. They will not discuss how the plans may or may not affect other aspects of the children's lives that do not directly affect the parents' parenting time. These conversations will be the right and responsibility of the parent making the plans for their own parenting time.

2.14 Neither parent will share with the children a trip, gift, etc. the other parent has informed them of unless they have written acknowledgement from the other parent that the children have already been told. The parents may respond should the children raise these things but will not ask questions so as to gain information that would appear to be intrusive or interrogative.

2.15 Neither parent will discuss any plans made by the other parent in any way that negatively affects the children's perception of the plans.

Right of First Refusal

2.16 Hank and Annie agree that it is in the children's best interests to spend time with the other parent rather than with a third party. Accordingly, if either of them cannot care for the children for a period that has the children waking up without the parent present for 2 mornings in a row, he or she will notify the other and give him or her the opportunity to care for them. If the notified parent cannot care for the children, the parent will make childcare arrangements at his or her own expense.

It is understood that it is a natural course of childhood to spend quality time with a grandparent, this will not be considered a trigger for Right of First Refusal. Meaning, grandparents wish to have quality time with the children and the parent scheduled to have parenting time is available.

If either parent is knowingly going to be unavailable for any reason to exercise Right of First Refusal, they will notify the other parent, prior to departure, of the duration of unavailability to avoid failed attempts to contact for assistance. This does not remove the obligation to inform the other parent of any emergency that may arise with the children during this time.

Right of First Refusal will require adjustments over time to reflect the lifestyles and schedules of the parents and the ages and schedules of the children. Negotiate a structure that works for your family and comfort of both parents and children.

2.17 The parent residing with the children at the relevant time will make the daily decisions affecting their welfare without interference from the other.

2.18 Hank and Annie will consult with each other on important decisions about the children's welfare, including decisions about the children's:

(a) major education,

(b) major health care,

(c) major recreational activities, and

(d) religious activities.

If the parties cannot agree, they will use the terms under the Dispute Resolution section to resolve the dispute.

2.19 If the children need emergency medical care while with one parent, that parent will immediately, after any calls for emergency care, notify the other of the emergency and that parent may attend. If the other parent is unable to attend, they will receive updates when new information, tests, procedures arise. Should either parent need to attend to a doctor for a non-emergency reason the other parent will be notified of resulting care and any follow-up appointments made immediately upon booking.

2.20 Hank and Annie may make inquiries and be given information by the children's teachers, school officials, doctors, dentists, health care providers, summer camp counsellors or others involved with the children.

2.21 Both parents may attend all school functions. The parents may attend parent-teacher meetings separately.

2.22 Hank and Annie have the right to receive significant information with respect to the children's education, medical care, dental care, and mental health care, including the right to receive report cards, and any other documentation pertaining to them.

It is the responsibility of each parent to obtain significant information, report cards, school calendars, etc. and it is not the responsibility of the other parent to provide same. However, if a parent receives information that they can reasonably conclude the other parent may not be aware of, they will, via OFW, provide the information including but not limited to trip forms, school correspondence, class work, etc.

Extracurricular Activities

2.23 Hank and Annie agree that the children have the right to be enrolled in at least one activity each season and will share in all costs of the activities equally, including fees and equipment/outfitting. The parent in possession of any outfit, equipment, or other clothing purchased as a shared cost will not lend, gift or donate without conferring with the other parent to determine if it can be sold or where it may go.

2.24 Hank and Annie agree that the responsibility of traveling to and from extracurricular activities, programs or other appointments and other such arrangements will lie with the parent responsible for the children at the time. If the parent with parenting time is unable to transport a child or otherwise ensure that a child attends an activity due to a work commitment, and is unable to make other arrangements, the other parent will be offered the opportunity to pick that child up at home and return them immediately after the event/activity not using this as an opportunity to extend time with the child without written agreement from the other parent.

2.25 If a parent is volunteering for a school activity during the school day, or that begins during the school day, that parent may attend regardless of which parent is scheduled to have parenting time.

2.26 If either parent becomes affiliated with a child's activity, team, etc. as, including but not limited to, a coach, assistant coach, and that parent will be fully engaged with the team throughout the event, they may do so. This does not apply to a 'parent helper'.

2.27 Both parents may attend any championship game, recital, etc.

2.28 If the parent dropping a child off is not staying for the activity, they will ensure that at the end of the activity they are easily located/seen by the child to ensure that the child is not wandering looking for the parent.

2.29 Hank and Annie agree to provide all schools, doctors, and program leaders the contact information for both parents.

2.30 Neither parent will enroll either child in any program or activity that infringes upon the other parent's time without written consent of the other parent. All activities and costs are to be agreed upon by the parents in writing. Should a parent enroll a child in an activity that is not agreed to by the other parent, the parent enrolling the child will bear the entire cost.

2.31 Both parents acknowledge that vacations and special occasions will arise during a child's enrollment in activities and will respect the parenting decisions made by each other without interference or expectations expressed either to the other parent, or the children.

2.32 Neither parent will act as an intermediary between third parties and the other parent, always deferring the third party to the parent.

2.33 The parent with parenting time on the first day of school will do all the shopping for back to school necessities and will purchase upon receiving written agreement as to cost from the other parent. Reimbursement will be made upon receiving a valid detailed receipt. This will include but not be limited to school supplies, backpacks, winter wear, indoor shoes, etc.

2.34 The cost of haircuts will be shared equally with written agreement and a valid, detailed receipt.

2.35 Should either child not have important items with them at transition, including but not limited to medical devices, medicines, schoolwork, seasonal wear, the parent responsible for the child going to the transition will bring the item to the school the next school day.

Mobility

2.36 Hank and Annie agree that they will live no more than 45km from the children's school before triggering a review of the parenting plan.

Travel

2.37 Annie will apply for any Canadian passport renewals for the children. Hank will sign the passport application. Passports will be provided to a requesting parent within 48 hours of a request backed up with an email.

2.38 If either parent plans a vacation with the children for more than 4 days, that parent will give the other a detailed itinerary at least 10 days before it begins, or immediately upon booking, including the name of any flight and flight times, accommodation, including address and telephone numbers, and details as to how to contact the children during the trip.

2.39 If either parent plans a vacation outside the Country with the children, the other parent will provide a notarized letter authorizing the children to travel if requested. The parent requesting a notarized letter will deliver it to a notary local to the other parent, pay any fees applicable and the other parent will attend and sign within 5 business days. The parents acknowledge that there must be reasonable expectations that the other parent is able to attend at the notary and will not make the request when the other parent is on a scheduled vacation time with the children.

2.40 If either parent refuses to sign a notarized letter or does not sign the letter in a timely enough manner so to as interrupt travel plans, the parent refusing to sign will bear any costs incurred to procure the consent, whether that be legal costs, travel costs, etc. unless the dispute is caused by an attempt to adhere to the Parenting Plan.

2.41 Neither parent will unnecessarily interrupt the other parents vacation time with the children with any non-emergency information and/or requests.

3. Medical and Dental

3.1 Both Annie and Hank will maintain the children as beneficiary of medical, extended health and dental coverage through his or her employment for as long as it is available to him or her.

3.2 Annie will continue taking the children to annual medical appointments with Hank having the option to attend any consultation appointments that discuss the children's needs or plan of care and Hank will inform Annie prior to if he plans to attend.

3.3 Hank will continue taking the children to dental appointments with Annie having the option to attend any consultation appointments that discuss the children's needs or plan of care and Annie will inform Hank prior to if she plans to attend.

3.4 If both parents attend an appointment as set out in paragraphs 3.2 and 3.3 of this Parenting Plan the parent with scheduled parenting time will take point on all interactions allowing the other parent to participate in discussions where necessary. If only one parent is permitted to engage or to participate/join, the parent with scheduled parenting time will take priority and the other parent will not offer themselves to participate/join.

3.5 If either parent is unable to attend a consultation appointment the attending parent will attempt to provide as much information as they recall within 24 hours and the other parent is free to contact the provider to get any further updates.

3.6 Both parents may attend a major medical/dental event i.e., getting braces, day surgeries, etc.

3.7 Annie will hold and maintain Health Cards, Birth Certificates and passports for both children, providing Hank with photocopies.

4. Dispute Resolution

4.1 If Hank and Annie disagree about a reviewable or variable term of this Document, they will try to resolve the dispute through negotiation between themselves.

4.2 If Hank or Annie seeks a change, he or she will give the other, in writing:

(a) notice of the proposed change,

(b) evidence supporting the proposed change, and

(c) any requests for information from the other necessary to determine the issue.

4.3 A request under section 4.2 will be answered within 10 days.

4.4 If Hank and Annie cannot agree within 14 days of the request for review or variation, they will participate in mediation with a mediator chosen on consent of them both to resolve the dispute.

4.5 The parties will share the costs of mediation equally.

4.6 If Hank and Annie cannot resolve an issue that has been the subject of mediation, Hank and Annie may then confer with their respective lawyers to settle what, if any, variation should be made.

4.7 Annie and Hank will consider the option of arbitration prior to taking legal action.

If no agreement has been reached through mediation or their respective solicitors within 90 clear days after notice has been given, either parent may apply to a court to have heard that disputed issue only.

TO ACKNOWLEDGE THEIR AGREEMENT TO THIS PARENTING PLAN:

______________________	______________________
Hank Willoughbethere	Date
______________________	______________________
Witness	Date
______________________	______________________
Annie Hasaway	Date
______________________	______________________
Witness	Date

Your Personal Notes:

Chapter 17

Parenting Coordination: Choosing Peace Over Power

When Support Needs Structure

At this point, we have walked through many of the challenges that come with parenting after separation. We have explored how conflict affects children, how to manage emotionally charged exchanges, and how to create and follow parenting plans. We have talked about tools, strategies, and even the emotional work involved in healing and rebuilding.

But for some families, even with all this insight and effort, the conflict does not settle. The same arguments resurface. The same patterns replay. The parenting plan exists, but implementing it is an uphill battle.

When this happens, a more structured form of support may be needed. Something consistent. Something that steps in where communication breaks down and provides real-time guidance to keep children out of the middle. This is where parenting coordination comes in.

A New Path Forward for High-Conflict Coparents

When separated or divorced parents find themselves repeatedly caught in conflict, even after finalizing a parenting plan or court order, it can feel like the journey toward stability has hit a dead end. Parenting Coordination offers an alternative route. It is not therapy, and it is not more litigation, it is a guided process that helps families move from conflict to cooperation.

This chapter explores what Parenting Coordination is, what it offers, and why many parents, particularly those in high-conflict dynamics, choose to participate. We will also look at what the process entails, how it can benefit children, and what trade-offs parents should consider before committing.

What Is Parenting Coordination?

Parenting Coordination is a structured, child-focused process that supports families in implementing and following their parenting plans. It is especially valuable in situations where conflict between parents continues even after legal agreements are in place. Unlike mediation, which typically ends once an agreement is reached, parenting coordination can remain in place for months or even years, depending on the needs of the family.

A Parenting Coordinator (PC) is often a trained professional in family law, social work, or mental health (preferably a combination of family law and mental health) who takes on a hybrid role: part educator, part coach, part arbitrator. Their job is to reduce conflict between the parents, help resolve disputes quickly, and protect the children from exposure to ongoing tension.

What Parenting Coordinators Do

At the heart of Parenting Coordination is the child's well-being. PCs work to lower the emotional temperature between parents and keep focus on what serves the child's needs. While their services vary depending on jurisdiction and the terms of the agreement, most Parenting Coordinators:

- Help parents implement existing parenting plans by clarifying responsibilities, addressing logistical concerns, and interpreting vague terms.
- Guide parents through communication challenges, helping them develop more respectful, productive ways of interacting.
- Resolve disputes as they arise, whether about holiday schedules, school decisions, or parenting exchanges.
- Educate parents on the impact of conflict on children and on effective co-parenting strategies.
- Make binding decisions on minor parenting issues, if authorized to do so, when parents cannot agree.

In many regions, the role is legally recognized and may involve elements of arbitration, depending on the contractual agreement.

What Parenting Coordination Is *Not*

It is important to understand what this process is not. Parenting Coordination is not counselling or legal representation. It is not intended to change custody arrangements or override major court decisions. Rather, it is a pragmatic tool for addressing day-to-day parenting struggles that, if left unresolved, can escalate into full-blown legal battles.

Why Choose Parenting Coordination?

For many families, especially those caught in a loop of misunderstanding, resentment, and reactive parenting, a parenting coordinator can offer essential relief.

1. Stability for Children

Children thrive in predictable, low-conflict environments. When their parents have a reliable way to solve disagreements, kids feel safer and more secure. Parenting coordination ensures that issues are addressed quickly and without drama, protecting children from witnessing or becoming caught in disputes.

2. Support for Parents

The job of coparenting after divorce is hard enough without ongoing battles over minor issues. A Parenting Coordinator offers a sounding board, a mediator, and, if needed, an arbitrator who can help resolve small disputes before they become major disruptions.

3. Fewer Court Visits

Most parents do not want to go back to court over every conflict. Parenting Coordination provides a faster, less adversarial way to reach solutions. For high-conflict families, it may also reduce legal fees over time by decreasing the need for motion filings and emergency hearings.

4. New Tools and Skills

Parenting Coordinators do more than resolve issues, they teach. Over time, parents learn healthier ways to communicate, set boundaries, and prioritize their children's needs over their own disagreements.

Key: Parenting Coordination is not about "winning" arguments it is about choosing a path that puts children's needs above the conflict.

What It Costs—And What It Saves

Parenting coordination is a private service and not covered by public legal aid or private benefits. The cost varies by provider, but it is usually shared equally between parents. Some contracts will state cost as proportion to income if there is an existing court order or agreement that stipulates this. Parenting Coordinators charge by the hour, and services may include meetings, emails, calls, and decisions rendered.

While these fees can add up, the value often lies in what parents do not have to pay for: court motions, lawyers, missed work, or the emotional cost to their children. For families in long-term conflict, the investment can ultimately lead to financial and emotional savings.

Empowering Children, Not Just Parents

One of the most underappreciated aspects of Parenting Coordination is the indirect but profound benefit to children. When a PC is involved, the child's world becomes more predictable, less tense, and more supportive.

Children benefit because:

- They no longer feel responsible for resolving their parents' conflicts.
- They have more consistent rules and expectations across both homes.
- They spend less time exposed to angry conversations, tense transitions, or emotional outbursts.
- They feel safer knowing their parents have a system in place for problem-solving.

In essence, Parenting Coordination helps children stay in their role as children, not as referees, messengers, or emotional caretakers.

Key: By reducing parental conflict, Parenting Coordination gives children space to grow without carrying the emotional weight of adult disputes.

The Trade-Off: Giving Up a Degree of Control

While the benefits of Parenting Coordination are significant, it is important to understand the authority a PC may hold. In many jurisdictions, if both parents agree (or are ordered by the court), the Parenting Coordinator may have limited arbitral power. This mcans that if the parents cannot agree on a specific parenting issue, such as the pick-up location or whether a child can join a sports team, the PC may have the authority to make the decision.

This can be difficult for some parents to accept. Giving another adult the power to decide what happens in your parenting life can feel like surrendering your parental autonomy. However, this is not about giving up your role as a parent. It is about recognizing that conflict, if left unchecked, can do more damage to your child than any compromise ever could.

Reflection Prompt: Think of parenting coordination not as a loss of power, but as a shift in how power is used. It is moving from a "me versus you" model to a "what works for our child" model, supported by a neutral guide.

Key: Choosing parenting coordination means choosing peace over power. It is a commitment to put the child's well-being ahead of parental pride.

What to Expect from the Process

Every parenting coordination relationship starts with a written agreement outlining the scope, authority, and limits of the process. Once in place, the process typically includes:

1. Initial Intake
   Each parent meets individually with the coordinator to share background, concerns, and hopes for the process.

2. Clarifying the Parenting Plan
   The coordinator reviews the existing plan to understand where conflicts are likely to arise and ensures both parents interpret it similarly.

3. Conflict Resolution Support
   As disagreements arise, the coordinator meets with parents (together or separately) to resolve issues and facilitate understanding.

4. Ongoing Support
   The coordinator remains available for continued assistance as new conflicts emerge, often helping families transition toward independence over time.

5. Arbitration (if agreed)
   If parents cannot resolve a dispute and the coordinator has been given authority, they may issue a binding decision.

Is Parenting Coordination Right for You?

Parenting coordination works best when both parents are committed to reducing conflict and improving their parenting relationship. It is particularly effective for families who:

- Have frequent disagreements about parenting time or child-related decisions
- Have difficulty communicating without hostility
- Want to shield their children from ongoing arguments
- Are tired of going back to court

It may be less effective if one or both parents are not willing to participate in good faith or if there are serious power imbalances that cannot be addressed within the structure of the process.

Final Thoughts

Parenting Coordination is not a silver bullet; but for many families, it is a powerful and practical tool to move beyond destructive patterns and into a healthier future. It does require courage, especially the courage to admit that help is needed and that some conflicts cannot be solved alone. But in making that choice, parents give their children the most important gift of all: the freedom to grow up without carrying the weight of their parents' unresolved issues.

Peaceful parenting after divorce is not a destination; it is a path. Parenting Coordination helps light the way.

Final Reflection Questions

1. **Where are the areas of conflict in my co-parenting relationship that remain unresolved?**

2. **What impact do these ongoing disagreements have on my child?**

3. **How do I feel about involving a neutral third party to help resolve parenting issues?**

4. **Am I open to learning new communication skills, even if it means stepping outside my comfort zone?**

5. **What concerns do I have about giving a coordinator decision-making power in some areas? How might I address those fears?**

6. **What would it mean for my child if there were fewer arguments and more collaboration between their parents?**

Your Personal Notes:

Conclusion:

What Endures

By now, you have walked through the many layers of coparenting after divorce, communication challenges, parenting plans, complex emotions, and the ever-shifting dynamics between you, your child, and the other parent. It is a journey that asks so much of you. And still, you are here. Reading. Reflecting. Showing up.

That alone says something extraordinary about who you are.

There is no single blueprint for post-divorce parenting. No perfect script to follow, but there is a path—yours. It will be shaped by trial and error, by compassion and courage, and by your willingness to keep learning and adjusting, even when things are not going as planned.

In high-conflict situations, where one parent refuses to cooperate or puts their own needs above the child's, the burden can feel impossibly heavy. And yet, the truth remains: one calm, steady, emotionally available parent can make all the difference. That parent is you.

When your child looks back someday, they may not remember every schedule change or heated exchange. But they will remember how you made them feel. They will remember the stability you offered when everything around them felt uncertain. They will remember the tone of your voice, the consistency in your actions, the way you refused to let conflict define your parenting.

And even if they do not say it now, they will carry that love and security with them.

Key: You do not need the other parent to change to be effective. You only need to remain grounded in your own values. That is your power. That is your peace.

Reflection Prompt: Healing doesn't mean forgetting what happened or pretending it was fair. Healing means creating something stronger within yourself, something unshakable, even when the storm rolls in.

So, wherever you are today whether tired, uncertain, hopeful, or somewhere in between, know this:

You're doing sacred work. Quiet, unseen, relentless work. And every boundary you hold, every hard conversation you navigate, every ounce of patience you offer, it matters.

It adds up.

It endures.

Most importantly, your children will feel the safety of that love, even on the days you think you are barely holding it together.

You are not alone, and you are more than enough.

Made in United States
Troutdale, OR
11/03/2026

56844658R00116